The Making of Mia

Searching for Belonging in Daycare,

Learning to Live a Less-Scripted Life

Sarah Ayers

The Making of Mia:
Searching for Belonging in Daycare, Learning to Live a Less-Scripted Life

Sarah Ayers Publications
Bellingham, Washington
www.sarahayerspublications.com

Copyright © 2022 by Sarah Ayers

All rights reserved, including the right to reproduce this book or any portion thereof in any form whatsoever. For information, address:
Sarah Ayers
sarah@themakingofmia.com
TheMakingofMia.com

Every attempt has been made to source all quotes properly.

For additional copies or bulk purchases visit:
TheMakingofMia.com

Editors: Tyler Tichelaar and Larry Alexander, Superior Book Productions
Publishing Coach: Christine Gail
Cover Design: Sarah Ayers
Cover Photo: Gabrielle Jewell
Interior Layout: kdp.amazon.com
Author Photo: Sarah Ayers

Cataloging-in-Publication Data is on file at the Library of Congress
Softcover ISBN: 979-8-88680-777-6
Hardcover ISBN: 979-8-88680-785-1

10 9 8 7 6 5 4 3 2 1
First Edition, 2022

Printed in the United States of America

Dedication

To My Father

Acknowledgments

Justin Ayers: "Thank you" simply is not enough to say. You have been my first love and an absolutely wonderful father to our three children. We have built so much together, and I will forever love you for your support and deep friendship.

Sherri Benedict: Thank you for being the director I needed most. You met me when I was about to give up on being an early learning provider. Your story and leadership is what made me realize I, too, could be an impactful daycare owner.

Rick Taron: Thank you for being my dad, my teacher, and a powerful example of integrity and humility. You are the greatest man of God I have ever known, and I am forever thankful for you.

To my mother: You are exactly the mother every girl needs. You are powerful and compassionate in a way most women never are. Your love for the Lord and His scriptures will forever be with me. You were the greatest example of all that God would have a woman be. Thank you.

Laura: Thank you for being my counterpart.

To each and every one of my sisters: What remarkable people each and every one of you are! Each of you is passionate about something. None of you have settled for being ordinary. In your own ways, each of you is changing the world for the better every day. Included in this list are my beautiful sister in-laws! You have brought so much joy to our family in being the loves of my brothers' hearts. You are all so unique and yet have so much in common. You are elegant, talented, and have such wonderful gifts.

To my dear brothers: I have not stayed in touch as I have intended over the years, but I admire each of you for the strength and kindness you have shown to those in your worlds and spheres of influence.

Richard Miller: You were the pastor to my husband and me when we needed spiritual leadership the most. It was such a great honor to learn from you. Your death from the coronavirus made me realize each day is a gift and our time truly is limited here on earth. Your life was lived in integrity and faithfulness to the Lord in an unwavering way that will forever be remembered.

Aunt Carol: We fell out of touch decades ago, but you were the friend and aunt I dearly needed when I had questions I was too embarrassed to ask my sweet mother. You spent hours talking with me on the phone, and you were the one who gave me the courage to move to New York.

Tyler Tichelaar and Larry Alexander, my editors: Thank you for taking the stories so dear to my heart and transforming them into a best-selling book. You truly are masters of your craft, and I hope many more aspiring authors find you!

Calliope and Rian: Thank you for bringing the joy and inspiration to my daycare that you have! Every morning you have a smile and a kind word. Thank you for saying "yes" when I asked if you would honor me with your family picture as the face of this book. Sometimes simply saying "yes" opens up a whole new world. May you be blessed for the light and love you bring to the world every day!

Contents

Introduction	9
How to Use this Book	13
On Children	17
Chapter 1 The Making of You	19
Chapter 2 The First Question	23
Chapter 3 Meeting Mia	30
Chapter 4 The Thoughtfulness of Alice	39
Chapter 5 The Popularity of Mia	46
Chapter 6 Moving on to Another Making	52
Chapter 7 Talking with Jenna	56
Chapter 8 Looking Inward, a Different Way of Being	62
Chapter 9 Alex, A Girl Who Belonged	66
Chapter 10 Looking After Morgan	71
Chapter 11 Caring for Marissa	77
Chapter 12 The Kindness of Miss Rose	84
Chapter 13 Brooke and Elizabeth, All But Sisters	94
Chapter 14 Angel, the Angelic Child Who Did Not Belong	99
Chapter 15 Summer, Daughter of a Determined Teenager	103
Chapter 16 Choosing Another Story, the Decision that Changed Everything	108
Chapter 17 Deciding to Continue, Choosing Belonging	112
Chapter 18 Rachelle, the Little Girl Who Got Hurt	115
Chapter 19 Brooke, Showing Kindness to a Teacher Who Did Not Belong	122
Chapter 20 The Girl Who Decided Being Different Was Okay	126

Chapter 21 Finding Your Safe Place	131
Chapter 22 Adult Conversations, Changing the Way We Interact	134
Chapter 23 Where Broken Hearts Go	137
Chapter 24 When You Decide to Start Another Chapter	149
Chapter 25 Malachi, the Baby with Two Stories	156
Chapter 26 A Boy She Loved Very, Very Much	169
Chapter 27 Taking the Time to Fly So High with a Charity	176
Chapter 28 Connor's Sister: Noticing Children Who Don't Cause Any Trouble	182
Chapter 29 Jessica, the Girl Who Didn't Have Enough	189
Chapter 30 The Words That Saved Me	195
Chapter 31 Finding the Reason for What Moves You On	199
Chapter 32 Tuesdays	202
Chapter 33 When Thinking Just Becomes Too Much	208
Chapter 34 First Thing in the Morning	213
Chapter 35 Having the Last Word	217
Chapter 36 What Do Memories Mean to You?	221
Chapter 37 What Does Moving Forward Mean to You?	226
Chapter 38 On the Other Side of the Rainbow	230
Chapter 39 To This Day	234
Chapter 40 When You Find Yourself in the Kitchen	242
Chapter 41 Stepping Off the Bus, Where Would You Go?	250
Chapter 42 The Biggest Compliment	261
Chapter 43 Active Listening Is One of the Hardest Lessons	265
Bonus Section	272
About the Author	274

"If you could write down and pass along one lesson you've learned, what would it be? If you could relay one message, what would it be? If you could provide one resolution…would you?"

— Sarah Ayers

"Everything I've done has had purpose and has been passionate and has been executed in the best way that I knew how. Maybe that's not the perfect way. Maybe that's not the easiest way. But it's the best way I knew how to do it."

— Julia Roberts

"If you believe in yourself and have dedication and pride, and never quit, you'll be a winner. The price of victory is high but so are the rewards."

— Bear Bryant

Introduction

There are so many reasons for picking up a book. I often pick up a book because the cover is attractive to me. Every part of the cover of this book I have chosen for specific reasons, so if you judge a book by a cover, you will not be disappointed!

My hope is you will feel like you know me, and you are known by me as you read through *The Making of Mia*. The point I hope to make throughout this book others have also made—that the best, most lasting learning happens through play. I have taken a different approach. The angle I have taken is not academic; if it feels so, I have miserably failed. My desire is that you will see my point on a personal and relational way. After all, isn't that what play is all about? Academia certainly has its place, but it isn't the way I want you to learn—I want you to learn play through my voice. I want you to have fun with it and to experience daycare as I have, coming to your own conclusions by the stories I share.

Regardless of who you are, I know one thing about you. I know you are much like me, continually searching for belonging and clarity. You also love a good story.

In these pages, you will read about heartbreak, disappointment, and wonderful moments of feeling loved and treasured. The sense of belonging changes everything. You will find yourself many times over in this book.

The story of this book is told through the stories of many of the little children I have had the honor of working with as a daycare teacher. The lesson I hope to teach the world is that learning happens in early education and, truthfully, throughout life. Our experiences make up who we are. My message is that life needs to be less scripted.

With so many daycare workers throughout the world, why read my story? Simply put, because it is my story, unique from every other because it is mine, but I think you, too, will relate to it because of the way I share it. We all have the same problem: We all need to be seen, and that is something you will discover throughout this book. In a loud and fast industry, so many people are unseen, uncelebrated, and not given the chance to truly blossom as individuals.

If I did not record my story in this book, my work, and indeed, I myself would simply slip away into nothingness. If you did not pick up this book, you would never have the unique pleasure of meeting Mia, Morgan, Jenna, Julia, Erin,

Summer, Brooke, and several of the men who floated in and out of our lives. Only two of the daycares I worked at are referred to by their real names. Some events are real, some are fictional, but used to illustrate real-life scenarios.

My dear husband and three biological children are only briefly named. Why leave such special people out? Simply put, this is not their story. In fact, this is the story of Sarah Taron, a young woman who is passionate about helping children learn and who is also fighting to find belonging. Sarah believed, even many years ago, that world peace was and is possible. She believed the world could provide affordable healthcare, offer funding for early learning, control its waste to ensure proper temperatures, and establish governments that respect and understand human life is precious.

Like Sarah, I believe even today that simple understanding is the key to a better world. Life would be better for everyone if we simply respected one another. But that is not what this book is about. This book is about the heart of a nineteen-year-old choosing her own path, of leaving and moving on, of dedication and commitment.

That's the premise. This book is simply about my journey, your journey, the boys and girls' journeys of learning and finding a place of being cared for and seen, though their situations are so different. Each story is important, even though some are shorter than others. None of them have truly satisfying conclusions. While that may feel frustrating, it is simply because that is the nature of childcare. I was encouraged to create satisfying endings, but I have chosen to leave them as they are so that you, too, may feel as I do: a bit lonely, but glad knowing that I did my best.

My hope is this book will speak to your heart and you will find yourself within the narrative because whether or not you are in the daycare industry, you are a person in need of play and discovery, and you are in the process of finding belonging whether you realize it or not.

I dedicate this book to you. It is not written for me; it is simply written by me. I dedicate it to you, and perhaps even more, to the children whose names did not make it into the pages of this manuscript.

How to Use this Book

This book is for you.

So many feelings, stories, thoughts, and experiences are in this book. I didn't realize how much was in me to tell until I wrote it! And now I see there is much more literary work for me to do in years to come.

So how should you use this book? What do I want you to take from it?

There are three goals I have for this book. First, to help you see the world through my eyes. Specifically, I want you to see the childcare industry, but also to have a window into my personal life. Nothing is written in spite or from a desire to pay anyone back for misdeeds. There are two people in this book who did many people a disservice, but their presence in my life made me into who I am, so in that way I am thankful to them. I have thought about not including them in my book, but to do so would remove the reasons behind so much.

The second goal is for you to give deeper thought to the main point of each chapter. I help you do this by giving you journal prompts. Of course, doing these exercises is not required, but they are a way for you to benefit further from my life and experiences. After all, this book is for you; it is not about me at all. Truly, I do believe everyone is a storyteller at heart.

The third goal is to give you a project at the end of every chapter that relates to the main point of that chapter's story. These projects range from creating a Pinterest board to encapsulate my favorite boss or writing a playbook for behavior management to finding a gluten-free Play-Doh recipe or setting up a nap room. My intention is to make *The Making of Mia* practical as well as an entertaining story.

My suggestion is to read the full book, skipping the journaling exercises and projects so you can just enjoy the stories. Then, go back and put in time to think about each lesson. I'd very much like to provide a workbook to purchase along with the book to make this book easier, but for now, that is something for the future.

I will start this book by sharing my favorite poem, "On Children" by Kahlil Gibran. "On Children" has been close to my heart through the years of raising my own three children. Then, I will include quotations from my favorite people and some random people who said something clever relating to what I want you to glean from each story. At the end of every chapter, I have one awesome recipe, song, activity, or a self-care practice that has proven true over my many, many years serving as an early learning provider.

At times, I will talk about some sad things gently and with some passion, but the feeling I want you to take away from my book is a refreshed, happy spirit, hope for the early learning industry, and perhaps even more, hope for global peace.

I have also added the beautiful bonus at the end of letters from mothers to mothers. My hope is to bring encouragement and real wisdom. For real belonging comes from family, not daycare.

One of the greatest gifts ever given to me was the love of writing. I have been journaling since I was a young girl. And, for that, I thank my dear mother, whom I refer to as "Mama" throughout the book. Mother and father are far too formal for me. And I want you to feel how special my parents have been to me over a lifetime of their love and shepherding. I pass that gift of journaling along to you in the form of journal prompts. Whether you see yourself as a writer, there is so much value in taking a moment to reflect.

But for now, I simply want to say, "Thank you" and welcome you to my heart and life as I share my most treasured memories as an early learning provider and a young woman setting out into the world to do something, anything, to help the world and bring peace to all I meet.

At the end of this book, I have included real and fictional pictures of personalities in the book, as well as photos of items and places of significance because I want *The Making of Mia* to feel real to you. Some other items I have added include our favorite clay recipe, a meal planning template, a daily planner, and a list of some storybooks that have continued to be favorites over the years.

Enjoy!

On Children

By Kahlil Gibran (1883-1931)

And a woman who held a babe against her bosom said, Speak to us of Children.

And he said:

Your children are not your children.

They are the sons and daughters of Life's longing for itself.

They come through you but not from you,

And though they are with you yet they belong not to you.

You may give them your love but not your thoughts,

For they have their own thoughts.

You may house their bodies but not their souls,

For their souls dwell in the house of tomorrow, which you cannot visit, not even in your dreams.

You may strive to be like them, but seek not to make them like you.

For life goes not backward nor tarries with yesterday.

You are the bows from which your children as living arrows are sent forth.

The archer sees the mark upon the path of the infinite, and He bends you with His might that His arrows may go swift and far.

Let your bending in the archer's hand be for gladness;

For even as He loves the arrow that flies, so He loves also the bow that is stable.

From *The Prophet* (Knopf, 1923). This poem is in the public domain.

Chapter 1

The Making of You

"It's important to raise your voice in things you feel passionate about and things that you know about. Don't raise your voice just to raise your voice if you have nothing behind it and don't know what you're talking about."

— Zendaya

It is commonly said that memory begins when a child's speech becomes solidified.

Sarah's earliest memory is the touch, texture, feel, and sound of her world. She felt secure and loved, and she remembers the colors red and white, the touch of wood, and the smell of soup.

The biggest event Sarah remembered was her mother being gone, of hunger, and her grandma saying her mother would return soon. "Soon" felt like a lifetime. She remembers carrying a baking sheet above her head, looking up at her reflection, and wondering what it would be like to fly to her mother.

Her mother did come back, and she remembers the smell of pancakes, of molasses, of peaches with cinnamon. And she realizes as she looks back that these were the smells that filled the house for the full week that her mother was gone away to have her fourth sibling. Sarah learned later that her grandmother had brought gifts with her and that the baking sheet she held over her head and walked around with was the freshly washed pan that her grandma had stacked pancakes on.

Sarah was well loved. She belonged, and she was carefully cared for.

Mommy had gone away for so long because local doctors would not accept her into their care; she had given birth to twins (because having twins before was a liability no doctor would accept), had an unattended birth, and subsequently, children were too much of a challenge in delivery for local doctors.

Sarah didn't know then that her gentle, always-smiling mother was a fighter for her family. Indeed, she was a warrior and advocate in a time when prenatal care was so misunderstood. She was fearless in a time of fear. Sarah's mother had a strength and power, a spirituality that is rare even today.

The first year Sarah remembers is 1992. That was the year another sister was born. By 1998, she had eight siblings.

"When are you going to be done? Don't you know you won't be able to take care of or get to know your children if you have more than three? It isn't responsible to have a large family. Do you even care? What are you thinking? Haven't you ever heard of birth control? Don't you know that you need two incomes? When are you going to be done?"

As I look back on my early childhood now from the third-person perspective, I understand my parents in a new way and appreciate the simplicity of our life then.

It really is interesting to imagine what it feels like to be someone else. That is something I really thought a lot about in those days.

I left home in 2004.

As I would walk by people on the street, as I went from bus to bus or walked to work, or wherever I went, I remembered the feelings I had when my mom went to Oak Harbor to have my sister Evie Grace. Even in my three-year-old mind, I knew she was coming back and how deeply she loved me. And, so often, even now, I remember that feeling of belonging and have tried to hold on to it.

Journal Prompt

1.) What is your very first memory? What was the texture, smell, and (most importantly) your first feeling? Sometimes I feel like the memory of the vinyl tablecloth with a bold floral print, the reflection of the baking pan I looked up into, and the smell of banana pancakes gave me the sense of adventure and security that I had throughout my childhood. I felt connected even when I was scared.

2.) Has there been a seemingly wildly inappropriate question that you have been asked throughout your life, like my parents were asked regarding the size of our family? Why do you think that some people think asking questions like this are okay?

Chapter 2

The First Question

> "Did I offer peace today?
> Did I bring a smile to someone's face?
> Did I say words of healing? Did I let go of my anger and resentment?
> Did I forgive? Did I love? These are the real questions. I must trust that the little bit of love that I sow now will bear many fruits, here in this world and the life to come."
> — Henri Nouwen

One of the first questions you are asked when you sit down for a job interview is, "Why do you want this job?" The answer for many is, "Because I really need to make rent, and you called me back." But, of course, your prospective employer needs to hear more (unless they are completely desperate), and that deeper, more detailed answer, really, is what this book is all about.

Employers in early learning programs generally require a cover letter in which you describe your early learning philosophy. The first time I was asked to describe mine, I was completely stumped. Only now, after many years in the field, do I have a firm understanding of my philosophy.

Children learn through play—that is my philosophy and will forever be how I approach early learning. Believe it or not, childcare programs have many branches. Some will say, "Yes, children learn through play, but…." The result of that "but" is that play and learning become manicured and created. I believe in real play, the kind of play we did as children, building things outside, bringing things indoors from our wanderings, this really brings richness to learning.

Children learn to count by putting things together that they have collected. They learn to subtract by then taking away from that group. Then by putting these things into groups, they learn division and multiplication.

When I was a child, I did not grasp various topics (especially math) with the high aptitude my siblings displayed. I did not learn through book work like my oldest brother, younger brother, and my beloved sister Evie Grace did. But I did understand being outdoors, and I understood baking. I learned multiplication tables and division through baking. And the freedom to play outdoors and work in the family garden helped my siblings and I remain healthy in mind and body. I would like to see that in the early learning world.

Right now, and in the past several years, we have seen a movement toward outdoor preschools. And while the idea of licensing those care programs is a nightmare for the licensing department in Washington State, I still believe it is possible. I would truly like to learn more about it and be a figure in championing it in some way—possibly even through this book and subsequent published works!

Some programs are so completely regimented it is impossible to go back completely to free play. But I truly believe changes, even though they may be small, can be made to allow children to simply interact with each other. Through this book, I tell the stories of five different care programs I have worked with in various capacities. Of these, I primarily use two to show contrast and the range of philosophies. But I have by necessity left out so many other types of programs. They are different not only in their philosophies, but also in how their administrations operate, the staff culture, and how the organization interacts with families. These factors are multiplied by two because the programs generally operate one way on paper and another day-to-day. Is that a bad thing? As is too often the answer: yes and no.

Growing up, my mom often quoted Matthew 5:37, "Let your yes be yes and your no be no." It was certainly not the only scripture my mom recited. She had multiple verses for everything, but this one has stayed with me. And I find it so hard to follow because it seems that answers can go either way depending on the situation.

My ultimate philosophy is that families and children should come before politics. Policies should be formed around the unique needs of the families in each unique community. Out of respect for the programs, I changed the names. I still relate their essence and mission and how I feel they fulfilled them for better or worse.

In 2010, I opened my own daycare, and aside from following the licensing rules of Washington State, it was also shaped by the experiences I talk about in this book. If you are reading this as an early learning provider with aspirations of creating your own program, I am so glad you have found *The Making of Mia*. If you are a parent wanting to understand the *early learning world*, know that these five daycares are not all there is, but know also that you can learn from my experiences.

Play is powerful, and dear ones deserve the chance to learn through it. Policies must be created to serve families and be written by people who have spent some time with actual children and families. With all my heart and soul, I believe such programs can and will be created.

As I write this book, I am caring for a dear little boy I will call Zathan. (His real name is so much cooler.) When he joined my program, he cried and cried for hours and hours and was happy only when I would sit with him. Zathan didn't know what to do with toys when I handed them to him. It wasn't that he wasn't interested in Tonka trucks, jumbo balls, or building blocks; he simply didn't know how to use them and had zero interest in figuring out how. He didn't want books to read or to color in either.

After three weeks or so in my program, Zathan is now able to play on the floor with other children, sharing toys and running around outdoors with everyone else. When he first started at Gooseberry Childcare, he would cry harder when we went outside or started a different activity. All he wanted was to be held constantly. By pick-up time, I was not feeling at all pretty and sparkly.

Every day, I encouraged Zathan to play, and I sat on the floor with him showing him how to use each toy. And bit by bit, he was able to interact with and join the children himself. After being encouraged to interact with the environment independently, his enjoyment of daycare increased hugely, as did his self-confidence.

Even at College Way Child Development Center (I talk about it later), which was very carefully run to adhere closely to the latest trends, I don't think Zathan would have so naturally moved into interacting happily with his environment. I believe part of the credit goes to the small size of our program and that I was able to make his sweet mom feel welcome and truly supported. My point, though, is not that every program needs to be small. It is that care programs and children should be allowed to be different from each other.

Before COVID-19, the big push in the state of Washington was for all daycare centers to mirror each other, kind of like chain stores. Strong proponents of cookie-cutter daycare would strongly deny they were trying to make them all the same, but for a provider who champions individuality, it was obvious that was the goal. That is why I have fought for individuality throughout my years as a daycare owner.

The recurring lesson throughout this whole book will be: learning, confidence, happiness, belonging, and positive development happen through play. I really want you to see yourself in the stories of each of these little children. You need play as much as these kids. Modern life is so busy and fast, and time is so managed that we simply have no room for creativity.

As one of my mentors says, we are not created to sit at desks most of our lives as we do in American society, spending time outdoors just a few days each year. We are meant to play and explore no matter what our age or job. It's not just the children and early learning providers who need to get outside, but every person everywhere.

Journal Prompt

1.) What can you do within your preschool classroom to make the hard questions from families less difficult?
2.) What could you change in your personal life to allow for more creativity?

Project

Sketch out or create a collage of the best and worst outfits to wear to a job interview. I have always struggled with what to wear to an interview.

Chapter 3

Meeting Mia

"Let us always meet each other with a smile, for the smile is the beginning of love."
— Mother Teresa

Although my name is Sarah, I have been called "Teacher," "Mommy," "Her," and even "That one." But whatever people have called me, I have always been loved by the children. Similarly, I've called some of the children and others in this book by different names, mainly to protect their privacy, but the name Mia is correct, though I changed the daycare's name so she couldn't be traced.

My first memory of Mia is the tone of her voice and the flip of her carefree, blonde, curly ponytail. She never walked alone; she always had her arms linked with two other girls, walking confidently around the play yard. While happy and full of energy, she was continually telling others they were not her friends anymore for this or that reason.

The teachers at Weber Street Daycare thought they ought to talk children through these situations. The children whom Mia excluded could use some shoring up. But the truth was, Mia was (and likely still is) a girl who was always noticed wherever she went because she was so full of energy and enthusiasm. She was confident, and it appeared she felt no lack of belonging. She had the essence about her that simply drew people in; they wanted to know what she was all about because that kind of enthusiasm is magnetic. And I think that is why she stands out so completely in my memory. I have such a clear picture in my mind's eye of her as an adult that it makes me smile. I am curious about what life choices she made in her growing up years and what type of adult that has led her to be.

Sometimes as I think of her, it seems that we had a lot in common. We both pushed outside of the lines, challenging boundaries, and found learning within play. The primary difference that I notice now, after giving myself intentional time to consider, is that she did it in a bolder way and didn't seem fearful at all. As I get older, I still push and challenge and am finding confidence that she was bursting with then!

Arm linked in arm, three four-year-old girls walked in a way that can neither be described as quickly or slowly. It was more of a confident saunter around a partially shaded play yard in a daycare that was not the happiest place to be.

Of the three girls, the one in command was in the middle. She was in the center of everything. Mia's curls were as animated as she was. Her stride was the essence of confidence. She was fully aware of everything around her.

Mia's mom was named Julia; I cannot recall her father's name, but that seems fitting since this book is not about him. It is about Mia's mom and the girls on either side of Mia. This book is also about me. It is not my story, Mia's story, or even her mother's, but the story of all of us together.

Each child has kindness in them, each has hurt, and each longs for one thing. And, you, in your own way, may long for that one thing as well. But, perhaps, you are one of those people who walk through life feeling secure in having rules and a script. If you are one of those people, I must go no further without telling you how jealous I have been of you throughout my life! Even now as I write this book in 2022, I am wishing I could be like you. I am at a crossroads of choosing whether to finally step into following the rules and be safe or to continue on my trajectory. Defying the script I have been taught would topple what I have built, forcing me to grow even more.

It is funny how each of these children's stories bring back a specific memory. I want to build a full day out of each memory and stretch it into a week, a month, and just continue from there to completely imagine everything, and one day, I may. The best stories are the ones that carry on and on long after the cover is closed and the last words have been read. So it is with the children who played on the dilapidated play yard of Weber Street Daycare. One day, I will write a book of short stories dedicated to each child, for they truly deserve that.

Mia's story revolves around being out in the play yard with the other children. Weber Street Daycare had an unusual play yard. The front was gravel with a chain-link fence and a metal climbing structure in the middle. The daycare was originally a neighborhood grocery store. It had two huge display windows and flower boxes at the entry. The back play area had a section filled with tire chips. But at Weber Street, they were real tires chopped up, not the mulch especially designed for daycare playgrounds. In the summer, they had a terrible smell, well, like hot asphalt. The rest of the play yard was burnt and dead grass with a couple of benches, but the teachers weren't allowed to sit down. There wasn't a lot of shade for the teachers or children either. This didn't bother Mia in the least. She brought as much energy and sass to the play yard as she did to the classroom. While of us teachers were uncomfortable, hot, and struggling to have a positive attitude, Mia seemed to be in a completely different headspace.

Mia and her friends were oblivious to this discomfort and pranced about the play yard talking in their self-important, involved manner. That is one of the most wonderful things about children—they have the ability to simply live inside moments. Adults are not able to exist in that way; we carry the weight of so much on our shoulders every day in a way children do not. I often wonder what they were talking about as they walked around the play yard. Did they talk about more than who was and wasn't their friend for the day? If they are anything like my daughter's junior high friends, that would be what they exclusively talked about!

In my mind, I can see clearly the two swing sets I spent a lot of time standing by. The playground duty I most got was pushing the kids on the swings. Even though most of them knew how to pump, I really did enjoy standing there, pushing, and talking to them. I felt included in their little worlds, and that was exactly where I wanted to be. It was, indeed, my safe place. I found belonging with them there, and even now after I have owned my own daycare for more than a decade, pushing children on the swing is still one of my favorite activities. It is so repetitive that it gives space for thought.

The life I had outside the chain-link fences of Weber Street Daycare was certainly not one I will ever allow my children to be in. But, at the same time, I have so much respect for my parents for allowing me to be there in Colorado. The apartment I lived in was so small and in an area of town where a grown man would be hesitant to walk the streets. But I never felt unsafe. I lived with the bare necessities, nothing at all fancy. The only places I went outside of work were the liquidation store for food, Goodwill for clothing, the gym, the library, and church. It was everything I needed. And now, as I write this book, the world is coming out of the coronavirus lockdowns, and I realize those are still the only places I go. It is so interesting to look back on my former life and compare it to where I am now after building so hard.

The aspect I did have in my life, there in Colorado, was community. Community is what makes anything possible. Any difficulty can be overcome when there is some kind of community. And, really, that is the reason I say throughout this book that my wish for people everywhere is not that they have a certain income level. If people find a way to have some sense of belonging, anything is possible.

Right now, I would like you to think of a time when you wanted to be liked more than anything else. Perhaps it was first grade when you had good memories of kindergarten, but knew "real school" started in the first-grade classroom. You were confident, but also scared. Or perhaps it was moving from sixth to seventh grade, or finishing high school and having no idea what came next. Life has so many transitions. Perhaps think even smaller to moments when you felt like your future rested on one thing alone—think of these small bits of time that change everything. And truly, after all this time, I do believe in small moments.

One moment at Weber Street Daycare determined that I would only see six months of Mia's making. But those six months left an indelible memory of her in my mind. It was the moment that got me fired. It was one choice, one turn, one look, and one response. Really, I left Mia's story because I misunderstood something. Perhaps that is why misunderstandings bother me so much.

My favorite activities with children in Mia's age group (four- to six-year-olds) included anything with glitter and glue. Normal teachers hate glitter and glue, but I love it…or did when I worked at daycare centers, not my own home. I can still remember the smell of the art projects we created with them and the equal trepidation and excitement as the kids dug into the activity. Mia went about these activities with thought or planning and managed to stay in control of the whole process.

When I started working at Weber Street, we had zero training, not even an orientation. As a matter of fact, I cannot even quite remember an interview. I think I was hired based on one call to the beautiful Miss Rose at Comfort Care (a wonderful childcare facility I worked at in New York before moving to Colorado) that got me the job. But in any case, I was not even shown around the classroom or given a schedule. Instead, I got a shrug of a welcome from the toddler teacher who told me Miss Julia would be there the next day to help me, but to watch out because she wasn't what she appeared to be.

Later, I found a tall, blue, wooden cabinet with all kinds of random craft supplies and three easels behind a pile of old mats. I came up with all kinds of fun from that cabinet. It held all sorts of paints, powders, sparkles, and paint brushes in various states of yuckiness which, after some soaking, became usable. There were also floor puzzles, carpet mats for cars, and even sorting cups. I even found an old curriculum book in there. And so, from all of that, I created a curriculum and a haven for myself.

Journal Prompt

1.) What do you prefer children and families call you? Do you like to be called "teacher" or does that make you crazy? I have always been fascinated by how passionate preschool teachers can be about what families call them. I think this comes down to us wanting to feel respected. Traditionally, early learning professionals haven't been given a lot of respect, and I think that is why what we are called is a sensitive subject.

2.) What makes an impression on you as a teacher?

3.) What activities freak you out as a teacher or parent?

4.) Write about a time when you found a hidden something like the blue cupboard and describe what you did with it. That cupboard really can be a metaphor for so many things.

Project

Describe yourself from the perspective of the children as I described Mia. And, to add an artistic spin to the project, draw yourself. Be creative and have fun!

Chapter 4

The Thoughtfulness of Alice

"The lonely become either thoughtful or empty."
— Mason Cooley

"You wouldn't believe the day I had."

Who knew that these words would change the trajectory of my life? But they did!

It was 2003, and my twin sister and I were students at Whatcom Community College—a community college in a small town no one notices or remembers for long. But it was the only college I attended, and I put in all the effort and determination I had in me. As a teenage student still enrolled in high school, the system granted me free admittance to this school. Although I had been enrolled at WCC for three quarters, I still hadn't found something I was truly passionate about, except for a keen interest in psychology. But everyone knows that psychology can't turn into a career in only two years of junior college.

When my twin sister, who was working as a babysitter at the local YMCA, excitedly told me about a little girl named Alice who had drawn a picture for her, I was enthralled. I wanted a child to care for me like that. And so, on that sunny Tuesday afternoon, I decided what I wanted to do with my life.

The thing about twins, though, is that there is a leader twin and a follower twin. One twin makes the rules and the other is supposed to adhere to them. No one likes a copycat, and I must say I was a copycat and continued to live in my sister's shadow. And here, in choosing our focus in junior college, she was adamant—having the love of the Alices of the world would be her blessing and honor.

In 2004, I graduated from WCC with my associate's degree in arts and sciences with a focus in psychology. I enjoyed getting my degree, and my advisor supported my decision not to change focus because my degree had higher level math and science requirements, which, were I to pursue clinical psychology, would more smoothly transfer.

But, unlike my other three siblings who were also in different stages of finishing community college, I didn't put in the time to apply for grants or sit still long enough to do the normal thing and continue my education.

My twin sister is so good about keeping old photographs on hand. She readily posts them on social media when someone has a birthday or anniversary. It is one of the things I admire about her.

It doesn't take a picture, though, to remember my college graduation. I had long, blonde hair I curled that day, with a middle ponytail, and I was so proud to be wearing the maroon cap and gown. I wonder about others' feelings about graduating from junior college. My younger brother didn't even go to his graduation from WCC because he thought it wasn't a big enough deal to celebrate. For him and my other siblings, it was just taking care of prerequisites before moving on to the real game. And even now, I don't know how challenging university was for them.

I didn't really know any of the other graduates because I spent so much time studying in the library. As cool as they may or may not have been, I didn't have time to be in any clubs, and I skipped out on as many group projects as I could simply because I was afraid someone might think I wasn't smart enough.

But on graduation day, I was truly proud of myself, and I think my mom was too. I remember standing with my favorite teachers, Ben Kohn and Carol Wilkinson.

Carol was my favorite psychology instructor and the reason I wanted psychology to be my major, and Ben Kohn was my German and humanities instructor. I remember him because he thought learning the material was far more important than test scores. One German exam was especially hard for me, and he sat with me through almost all of it, prompting me until I found the correct answers. To this day, I remember many of the words and the grammatical structure because of his guidance. I have often wanted to be the Carol to children who need something to be captivated by and the Ben to children who struggle to learn but are determined to do so. Good teachers are not afraid to step outside the rules and give extra support when it will be helpful in the long run. Lazy students are not the same as students who struggle to understand.

Even as I write this, I think about going back to school to see what it would be like as an adult. Even if it were still hard, I now have a system for working through challenges and a frame of reference for challenges, plus a whole new set of motivators.

I needed to find something in the world. I didn't know what it was, but I felt it wasn't where I was. I was in Northwest Washington, I was nineteen, and I was in love. I was in love with the idea of there being more.

Not unlike Mia, I was looking for a sense of belonging. Being raised in a large family with a sister who knew all the answers, I did not feel I had a place or a need to be there. And so, that fall evening after graduation, I decided it was time to move on.

My family did not like the idea. Whether conveyed directly or indirectly, I believe every child is raised on some core messages. And mine centered on: Girls are to stay at home until they are married. My idea did not follow that very simple expectation.

At the time, my twin sister had a suitor who had been interested in her for two years. I also had such a person: Peter. He is not a part of this story and will not be mentioned again. But it is important to mention him so you know I was not overlooked in my family. There was a plan for me, I certainly had not slipped through the cracks. I was (and am) taken care of. Though my parents had nine children, they watched and cared for each of us.

As children, we see our parents in such a one-dimensional way. My parents are both in their late sixties as I write this, and every time I spend time with them, I simply watch and observe how they are with each other and their outlook on the world. They see it in such a clear, agreed-upon way. I wonder if the world is ever confusing or scary for them as it has been for me at times. They have a kind of certainty about everything they do.

My parents have always stood strongly together, but now I also see how much they care for each other. They are so much more than pillars of fortitude; they take care of each other and truly enjoy life in their own way.

So many demands are put on marriages, so many expectations that are truly based on nothing. I wonder what would happen if couples only allowed themselves to focus on what was important to them and lived life though that lens. Would marriages have more longevity?

And, for the interest of this book, if we could decide in our preschool classrooms throughout the world what our top three values were, would children's early learning experiences be stronger?

Journal Prompt

1.) How can you foster thoughtfulness in your classroom?

2.) Do you make a point to notice thoughtfulness in students and celebrate it, or do you have the propensity only to notice negative behavior?

3.) What does "slipping through the cracks" mean to you personally, and how can it happen within the early learning setting?

4.) What do you think of Mason Cooley's saying, "The lonely become either thoughtful or empty?" From what I've seen, I think that is really true.

Project

Find a way to show parents that you think about their children. For me, that means texting them with a positive report of some kind during the day. It makes a world of difference to some parents. Don't let practicing this interrupt classroom time, but find something special to do to be encouraging during what is normally a stressful time for parents.

Chapter 5

The Popularity of Mia

"A deep sense of love and belonging is an irreducible need of all people. We are biologically, cognitively, physically, and spiritually wired to love, to be loved, and to belong. When those needs are not met, we don't function as we were meant to. We break. We fall apart. We numb. We ache. We hurt others. We get sick."
— Brené Brown

"You can't be my friend today," was said in the most aloof manner every day with a toss of blond curls coming from an easy, high ponytail. This grand swoosh of hair punctuated a daily, if not hourly dismissive pronunciation. Mia's friendship circle was indeed an envied place to be. It was, however, not a secure place. No, it was certainly not a place of belonging, but it was one of honor.

When I first met Mia, I was struck by her confidence and poise, and by Miss Julia. Julia was not only Mia's mom, but she was also the most fawned-over teacher at that small, unhappy daycare in Colorado Springs.

Miss Julia had long dark curls, was very slim, and a little shorter than me. Her face was clear, with only a hint of deeper concern. Julia played in a local jazz band. She seemed untouched by the director's gloomy demeanor, which seeped into the hearts of every other teacher there. She was given all the time she wanted to work on a large painting of Puff the Magic Dragon, which was to be the main attraction at the soon-approaching preschool graduation.

No other teacher at that school had a clear, joyful face. None had inspiration and interest in their eyes aside from me and Miss Julia. And that is what attracted parents, children, and teachers to us. The director, however, did not take to either of us. An older teacher, Miss Gina, told us our days were numbered unless we toned it down.

Miss Julia was something special. But she was able to fade into the background and be unseen by the director, Miss Doris. I was not, so I got fired from Weber Street Daycare just as Miss Gina had warned.

Miss Julia and her beautiful daughter Mia continued on at Weber Street Daycare in Colorado Springs, Colorado. I often wonder what became of them. Perhaps if Mia hadn't been a source of income for the daycare, Miss Julia would have been fired as well. I wonder if Miss Julia was happy there, or if it was just a paycheck. Maybe that was the key. I was, in those early years, always putting so much of myself into everything I did. Only in the last three years have I learned how to work in a more sustainable way.

Wondering what happened to Mia and Miss Julia is what inspired me to write this book seventeen years later. I still wonder what became of Mia and what went into making her.

Since Weber Street, I have raised hundreds of children as an early learning provider and three beautiful children as a mother. This book is about them. And, truthfully, it is also about the making of me.

One of my favorite mottos is, "Be kind to your past self; they brought you to where you are now." I have gone far and grown in many ways. My heart has been broken and built again. This is my story, this is your story, and this is Mia's story.

As I take time to think back on my time in Mia's life, I remember how entirely left out I felt. Her mom, Miss Julia, invited me a couple of times to listen to her jazz band play. I never had a date, and I couldn't afford nice clothes or anything more than tea. While everyone was dancing and smiling, I was alone.

An interesting part of the story of Miss Julia and Mia is how it highlighted what was important and noticed by the parents at Weber Street Daycare. When I joined the program in May 2006, we were nearing preschool graduation. The big project Miss Julia was working on was painting a huge backdrop and teaching the kids songs to perform at graduation.

Working on that project excused Miss Julia from her regular duties, leaving us shorthanded. Miss Doris was more concerned with gaining the parents' admiration and affirmations than adhering to the required ratio of teachers to students in the State of Colorado. As I've seen, administrators like Miss Doris strictly enforce the rules on others, thinking themselves outside, if not above the regulations.

If it were any other teacher, I would have resented this favored treatment, but Miss Julia was so kind and sweet it felt like an honor just to be teaching in the same program as her.

The graduation was a huge success, and Miss Julia was praised by every parent. After that, though, the director lost interest in Miss Julia, and she was back to the regular duties of a daycare teacher.

50

Miss Gina, the other preschool teacher, did not like Miss Julia at all and was continually gossiping about her. But I liked Miss Julia and enjoyed the six months I was allowed to teach at Weber Street Daycare before I was fired in November. Despite the warnings, I didn't see it coming.

Truly, even though I loved the children at Weber Street Daycare, I felt no sense of belonging. And, while it was sad to leave Mia and the other children, I was glad to move on to God's Light Childcare. God's Light is a school in Colorado Springs, and I would be honored to visit it again.

Journal Prompt

1.) Do you notice children in your classroom who are especially popular? If so, what makes them popular? Have you noticed yourself interacting with them differently just as the children do?
2.) Have you felt happy in a place, but realized you felt no sense of belonging in that place?

Project

Try behaving like the popular four-year-old in your personal life and notice how people treat you. You need to be in a certain mood to pull this off, but it is a lot of fun.

Chapter 6

Moving on to Another Making

"Bad things do happen; how I respond to them defines my character and the quality of my life. I can choose to sit in perpetual sadness, immobilized by the gravity of my loss, or I can choose to rise from the pain and treasure the most precious gift I have—life itself."
— Walter Anderson

"When you get to know her better, you will understand why."

It's interesting when beautiful people, who seem to have everything together including personal peace, really do not. Miss Julia was interesting in this sense. And, indeed, I figured out later, her personal life was very much what made Mia Mia—Mia's mom needed to be in control, and her father couldn't take the pressure of that. And so Miss Julia had the same flip of her high ponytail that Mia had. She had the indignant confidence and pride that led her to becoming the single, glamorous, determined mother she was.

The making of Mia was her mother, a beautiful lead singer of a local jazz band, the favorite daycare teacher, impervious to the hatred of the director of Weber Street Daycare. I often wonder what happened to Mia and Julia.

But more importantly, what happened to me after I lost the position at Doris's daycare there on Weber Street. Well, I moved on. It didn't take long to find another daycare eager to add Sarah Taron to their payroll and team of teachers.

I simply moved on as I had done three times before, twice in New York and once in Colorado Springs. Staying was not my way. Moving on was my way. From one center to another, from the raising of one group of children to the next, I would be part of the program for six months to a year and then move on and on.

What caused me to move? I was searching for belonging.

Even though I left Mia and never heard what happened with her, I continued to be part of her story by providing care to little girls and boys in different places over the next decade.

As I researched this book, I checked on Weber Street Daycare. My research showed that they had closed because their license was not renewed. That really piqued my curiosity. I wanted to know more and to…well, maybe find what happened. But then I decided it was better I remain curious and let my imagination tell the rest of the story.

And so, I will remember Weber Street Daycare as a random daycare in the middle of a random neighborhood, but it really was more than that. A lot went on within my heart when I worked there.

This book will tell the stories of ten more girls, and within their stories, many more stories of little children whose lives will forever touch my own and, hopefully, your heart will be changed as mine was. Every child matters, and they will forever be in my heart.

Journal Prompt

1.) Are you one to move on and on like I was in my earlier years of teaching daycare? If so, why do you think that is?
2.) If you found belonging from within yourself, would that have changed things? Looking back, I feel it would have for me.
3.) Were you ever forced to move on, or do you feel you remained in control of your life even at a young age? I often wish I could go back and try again, or

even more, go back as my thirty-six-year-old self and address Miss Doris who fired me.

Project

Write a letter to the grown-up version of a child you cared for, telling them they are loved and all the good things you wish for them. Simply doing that has given me so much peace. It makes me a little sad each time a child moves on from my program. Writing a letter, even though I will never send it, always gives me peace. Plus, it is kind of fun to imagine whom these children might have become.

Chapter 7

Talking with Jenna

"Too often we underestimate the power of a touch, a smile, a kind word, a listening ear, an honest compliment, or the smallest act of caring, all of which have the potential to turn a life around."
— Leo Buscaglia

"If you talk to her, you will just get sucked in, and then she will never stop. She won't nap, and then you know what will happen with the day."

For some reason, I have always remembered those words and wondered what would have happened if I had let Jenna trick me into letting her get out of naptime. Would I have learned more about her and perhaps made her feel more at home in her life? Perhaps. Was naptime that important? Not really to me because, truthfully, I craved conversation, and I think maybe Jenna did as well.

I remember Jenna also because of her birthdate: September 11, 2001. She was four years old when I met her, and I always wondered if she knew what was so special about her date of birth. She probably didn't as a preschooler. She understood a lot, though. And I remember a lot about her young self.

"He broke my mama's heart, but she broke my daddy's heart too." The other daycare workers always giggled when she said this while telling stories. It broke my heart not only for her, but for the conversations she had likely overheard that brought her to say such a thing.

Jenna was a very thoughtful girl. She was observant, and that is what made her so compelling and fun to chat with. In those days, I very much appreciated having someone to listen to. I was not in as much of a hurry as I tend to be now.

Jenna was a little girl who often walked around the play yard with Mia and sat with her at group times indoors doing craft projects. While Jenna had blonde hair, she had a different sense about her. She was usually not the one loudly declaring others were not her friend. Jenna was inclusive and often thought about her father's happiness.

And yet, from the teachers' perspective, Jenna's dad was not a very nice man at all. He drove a luxury car and was dismissive of everyone. But more than that, we didn't like him because his wife was the younger version of his ex-wife. While flirting with dads is a favorite pastime of daycare teachers, none of that was happening with Jenna's dad.

But Jenna felt a sense of belonging and love in that household. I wonder where she is now, but I feel sure she is happy and very well taken care of. It is hard to know what turns life might have taken, but I feel a general sense of peace about Jenna that I simply don't have with little ones like Morgan, whom we will meet in Chapter 10.

Whenever a child I am worried about leaves my care, my husband says, "It's okay; they will be okay. Life does go on, and they don't truly need you." While that sounds mean to me at the time, I have learned it is true, and I cling to that truth.

They will be okay as certainly I will.

Death, sadness, and lack of belonging are real in every single life, mine included. As I write this, one of my dear friends is dying of the coronavirus. I often wonder how all these children I have cared for are doing during this global pandemic. The truth, though, is I did the best I could when they were in my care, and their lives are not mine.

Jenna's father and mother divorced when she was three. He soon married a woman ten years younger with the same hair color, eyes, and classy, Audrey Hepburn-style of dressing. Both women were absolutely stunning—the only obvious difference being one woman was younger than the other. As with everything, there was more to the story, but in our daycare world, we disliked Jenna's dad for his arrogance at school and our perception that he had left his wife for a younger version.

I can only guess Jenna's parents were on a similar journey to mine. At the time, a drama involving a "love" triangle was unfolding that would lead to my own heartbreak. Miss Doris was the problem, of course. She did not appreciate me talking to the bus driver, who was married, and whom I thought chatted with all the daycare teachers.

I know there may be a level of dissatisfaction for the reader when I talk about possible sexual interactions because nothing actually happens. I am not trying to be coy or cryptic. I was entirely unaware of what was going on with the bus driver or with many other male parental figures. And, by God's grace, I was always safe, intact.

I later found out that Jenna's dad ignored every other teacher and sought opportunities to interact with me. I also found that Miss Doris hoped he would notice her—even though he was married. I could do nothing about the situation because I was fired the next week following a field trip to the zoo. On that outing, he helped me keep an eye on the four children I was responsible for, and I wasn't aware that the director was upset or watching. In fact, thinking back, I don't know how she knew because she wasn't there. It is one of those things that simply doesn't matter anymore.

It is possible that Miss Doris had found belonging at Weber Street. Indeed, it may have been a place of belonging that she never wanted to have. She belonged where she had been for twenty-five years as the director of a thirty-year-old daycare that was only licensed for fifty kids. It was a job with no room for promotion. She was an angry woman, but she was also reliable. The owner knew Miss Doris belonged. Perhaps she needed to fire me because I was new and fresh, or because the bus driver had a crush on me. Who knows? In any case, I am thankful to Miss Doris.

Journal Prompt

1.) Write an alternative ending to this story.

2.) Would you quit before Miss Doris had a chance to fire you?

3.) How does it make you feel when you hear children talk about heartbreak?

4.) Do you have a mantra you tell yourself when you are having a hard time with something?

Project

Think of a theme song to go with the unfortunate situation I found myself in, a triangle with two adults who didn't see each other in the way the other wanted. The song I think of is "True Colors," written by Billy Stenberg and Tom Kelly. Something about the sound of Phil Collins' soft, melancholy, yet cheerful voice speaks to how I felt in those days. I desperately wanted to belong at that little yellow daycare with the odd blue art closet. I know it may be a bit weird to think of life's situations having theme songs, but I do!

Chapter 8

Looking Inward, a Different Way of Being

"With the new day comes new strength and new thoughts."
— Eleanor Roosevelt

Each time I left a program, I was hired by another daycare within two weeks. As a daycare owner of thirteen years, I wonder how I was able to find jobs so quickly. Was there a huge shortage of childcare professionals in Colorado Springs then as there is now in Washington State with the pandemic? And, where and how did I find all those jobs?

A week after being fired from Weber Street Daycare, I was walking home late at night with my bags of groceries when I stopped for a moment and looked in the windows of the daycare from across the street. Until then, I hadn't given myself a moment to be sad about not being with Mia anymore. It was then, looking in at my old classroom, that I felt deeply lonely. I missed Jenna, Mia, Alex, and all the other children I had cared for. I missed the preschool classroom, the weird smell of the cleaning solution we made every morning as part of the morning routine before families arrived, and the cook's endless availability for gossiping with whoever took their lunch break near her kitchen. I missed the blue closet with its endless supply of half-used art supplies and their limitless creative possibilities. I missed everything but the bus driver and Miss Doris.

But, over all these years, I have been grateful for Miss Doris. Her anger and resentment, even her brand of belonging, taught me something very important. She taught me I never wanted to belong or simply be the way she was.

Miss Doris has caused me to look inward over the years to ensure I am not where she was. And if, for even a moment, I feel as though I am becoming resentful, I make a change and find a way to challenge myself.

Those days were also full of excitement—a time of friendship with a dear friend I would always remember and memories created that I hold especially close in hard times, now nearly two decades later. Think about the positive things you can hold on to even in hard times. As I get older, I realize we can find belonging in many places, even if they aren't normal or acceptable. But one of the greatest skills is to find belonging within yourself.

Back then, at the end of every day, I would take my journal from beside my bed and write at least two pages of my feelings, thoughts, and plans for…well, I am not sure what for. Back then, I didn't quite live by a plan. I still have all those journals, but I simply don't know what to do with them.

In my journals, I talk about the struggles and challenges of living on the move. I don't read them because I don't want to completely remember loneliness. And yet, when my twin sister or my husband ask why I keep them, I don't quite know. I have said I keep them for someone to read when I die. It is important to leave your voice in some way in the world after you're gone.

My journals were a way of looking inward, as is writing this book. I hope you will be inspired by it to write your own book. You don't need to be an awesome writer to be an author; you just have to have an open heart. If I were not writing this book, all these stories of all of these children would simply evaporate, as indeed they have partially. As I write, it feels as though I am snatching small moments from the past, grabbing and preserving their stories from the recesses of my memory. For memory is such a fickle, changing thing. This has also been a fear of mine: What if my telling of my story, which includes my family, isn't in accordance with other people's versions of it? When I've expressed this concern, my sweet husband has told me, time and again, "Then they need to write their versions of that story."

You own your own story; you lived your own story. And so, I look inward because it is the best way of being and telling my story to the world.

Journal Prompt

1.) Can anger ever have a positive spin?

2.) Can we incorporate play or curiosity into a hard situation?

3.) If so, what could we do and how would the outcome change?

4.) Do you ever wonder how a situation may have been different if you were an older version of yourself?

5.) If you could go back to a given situation, what would you do differently?

6.) How do you feel toward people who have wronged you?

7.) What do you do when you need to process your past or work through a challenge?

Chapter 9

Alex, A Girl Who Belonged

"A feminist is a person who believes in the power of women just as much as they believe in the power of anyone else. It's equality, it's fairness, and I think it's a great thing to be a part of."
— Zendaya

"Go out! Back up, back up—its Alex's turn!"

This was shouted across the play yard often. If a four-year-old can be a badass, then that badass's name was Alex. Alex was badass because she was entirely confident. She didn't feel the need to be girly or to play only with boys. She played with whomever she wanted to play with and was welcomed wherever she went. Alex didn't search for a group to fit in with. Brené Brown talks about belonging in many of her books, saying it happens when we find it within ourselves. I truly believe some children can find it within themselves when they have parents who have reached a sort of equilibrium in their relationship with each other.

Alex was a student at Weber Street Daycare just as Mia was. It wasn't a large program, but I don't have a memory of the two girls really playing together. I guess the reason is the same as it is for many adults; you simply don't have a need to interact with someone who has such an entirely different agenda than your own.

Alex's games and interactions weren't really about hierarchy at all, just a girl having fun with whoever wanted to play.

I chose to call this book *The Making of Mia* rather than *The Making of Alex* because I see myself in Mia's group. I was Jenna, the girl who was so close to Mia, just trying to break into Mia's level of coolness. Mia was behind her own making and contributed to everyone else's. Alex's making and sense of belonging came from her family. Her preschool friends simply bobbed up against that—they weren't needed to define her.

Alex had an arm like you would not believe when it came to softball. If she was in your lineup, your team was going to do very well. Everyone knew it, and everyone watched out for her. And the children would choose her first for their team if they had the chance.

Alex didn't need us teachers to help her move into playing with different groups like we had to do with other children. Alex seemed to come programmed or taught how to play with others. She was kind, but not introverted like Alice or Elizabeth. I am absolutely fascinated when I consider the children I have worked with. They are all so entirely different.

But Alex was not popular like Mia. She was made out of something else. But unlike Mia, Alex belonged. She had nothing to prove to the other children or to the teachers. Alex didn't tell others they couldn't be her friend for the day. She didn't push ahead in line and clamber to sit by this or that child at story time. She didn't chatter at naptime. By naptime, Alex was absolutely ready for the hour and a half of sleep our schedule demanded.

Alex's story in this book is not long. I mention her so you understand not every child who has been in my care was desperately searching for a place. Alex had hers. Alex's mom adored her, but didn't idolize her. Her father was popular with all the teachers, but never seemed to notice. He was indeed a family man, and Alex knew he was her biggest fan.

As I write about the many children I have worked with, my mind keeps going back to little Alex. Why is she so important to this book when her chapter is so short? I really think the answer is simply that she had already found the belonging that many other children never find.

Of course, that is only the perception of a teacher who got to work with her for six short months. Her dad did not seem to notice the many attempts teachers made at flirting. And her mother always seemed peaceful and sure of herself in a genuine way that not every mom possesses. Often, daycare providers see parents at their best and worst, but with Alex's parents, I didn't really see a worst. I continue to think of her just as I think of every child I encountered, wondering what I missed, what I didn't see, and then, of course, who she became over these many years.

Journal Prompt

1.) If belonging was dependent on a child's situation, do you think a child in a split family could feel it?
2.) Would you interact with someone like Alex differently than you would Mia?
3.) Do you think as I do that it is fair to interact with each child differently since each child has different needs?
4.) What draws you to children?
5.) What do you notice in Alex's story that is different from the other children's stories?

Project

The whole point of this book is that the best learning happens through play and belonging is developed when teachers do not manufacture situations. Alex really is the perfect example of this. But, just for argument's sake, write a lesson plan for teaching the Alexs of the world. (I do believe in the curriculum, just not to the point that it makes relationships fake.)

Chapter 10

Looking After Morgan

"Sometimes you can find peace of mind by transferring yourself to different situations. They're just reminders to stay...calm."
— Yves Behar

Morgan's heels kicked gravel across the playground as she spat words from her angry heart and mouth that even she could not understand the reason for. She was exhausted, confused, and heartbroken. She longed for love, but the only thing she knew how to get from adults was annoyance and then, shortly after, anger. She didn't know how to be sweet. Her hair clung to her head and neck. It was never in a high ponytail or carefully curled. Her face was always dirty, her knees were always grubby, and an unpleasant smell hung over her. She couldn't remember ever having freshly laundered clothes or new shoes.

Morgan's name was always said unkindly. The last time she saw her mother, her mother was drunk. The last time Morgan's father saw her mother, the woman was dead. Her dad had never been the same, and the only time he slept was when he was either drunk or so tired that he looked dead. He broke windows and hit walls. They had a lot of broken things in their single-wide trailer.

A lot of things cause post-traumatic stress disorder (PTSD). For Morgan's dad, it was the sudden, horrible loss of his girlfriend, who was the mother of his only child. The way social workers tell stories are so very different from how people experience the traumatic events. After a few weeks of being among my clientele, Kenneth (Morgan's father) told me he blamed himself. His girlfriend died drunk in the car of another guy, who was also intoxicated. They slammed into oncoming traffic. Kenneth thought somehow he could have kept her from that situation. But the truth was, he later admitted that Morgan's mother hardly ever came home and was not interested in him or her baby. He thought she would change as she got older, but nothing changed.

When Morgan was five and a half, her father was on the verge of losing custody of her. He had done the best he knew how. He never meant to be a single dad. He had been the guy with good intentions whom bad luck simply happened to.

Morgan did not understand what was happening with her dad, just that her mother's death made her dad sad. He had started crying more than yelling, and that made her feel even more lost than ever before. She wanted to help him, but it seemed there was nothing she could do anymore either.

And then, one day, things changed. She was removed from the daycare she had attended since she was four years old. Morgan wasn't sure why she never went back to that daycare. Kenneth didn't talk to her about it at all. They simply stopped driving to town. She spent her time with her confused, sad, angry, and lost father. She didn't feel loved there, even though the teachers often had kind words for her, but at that daycare, Morgan's belly was full and she was allowed to sleep. The children didn't want to play with her, but children had often been like that.

After Morgan had spent a week at home with her dad, the social worker who had been working them since her mom had died called with news. Morgan had been accepted at a daycare, and she could attend while her dad looked for work. Morgan was nervous about starting at another daycare after being kicked out of her old one without understanding why. But she was happy to go somewhere she would have food and safety—and a break from her broken father who had started to drink again.

The daycare Morgan joined in early June was the one I had opened at twenty-three years old. Both Morgan and I were at new, fresh points in our lives. She was finally at a daycare that took time to know her as a little girl in need of being loved for who she was. And I was a brand-new business owner. We both had old habits and experiences that built who we were, but we were giving life another go!

Kicking gravel and yelling is what had worked for Morgan in the past. It freaked the teachers out and, ultimately, whatever she wanted was given to her. Sometimes, she didn't even know what that thing was aside from a release of anger.

At my daycare, there were no other children Morgan's age. There was no one she felt she needed to compete with, no one for her to perceive as judging or being mean to her. Morgan was finally at a place where she could relax, where meals were regular, and where she always had a chance to catch up on sleep.

Life is hard for a young woman on a mission, just like it is for a girl with the cards stacked against her before birth. Both Morgan and I were (and hopefully she still is) people who wanted to lead and define our own futures. Though others tug at us, shouting our names, demanding we conform, we cannot be ruled. We are simply beings who belong to another world, a world of our own making.

And so is Mia. This is Mia's story, Morgan's story, and my story.

"They are going to take her away from me. I just know they are going to take her away."

Even as he said this, Kenneth was unable to maintain eye contact with me. He always shifted from foot to foot and had a way of darting his eyes around, constantly looking miserable. But that day, he looked especially devastated. It was as though I were the last person he felt he could trust. And with every part that was left of his troubled mind, he firmly thought I could help him. Truthfully, the only help I could give was what I have always been able to: a safe place to play and learn from 7:30 a.m. to 5:30 p.m., Monday to Friday, closed bank holidays.

Morgan left my daycare in September. She was taken from her dad's angry, broken home that cold September morning and never returned. I never found out what happened to her aside from the state deciding her father was no longer fit to be her father. His anger and drinking had simply gone too far.

Journal Prompt

1.) Morgan terrified most teachers. What would you do if a child who intimidated you joined your program?

2.) Do you think compassion for a child is possible in this kind of situation? And if so, what kind of a difference do you think it would make?

3.) Have you developed practices that enable you to deal with especially chaotic situations? If not, what might you develop?

Project

Create a chart of behaviors and consequences or reactions that would make the situation better. This has actually been a challenge for me.

Chapter 11

Caring for Marissa

"How far you go in life depends on your being tender with the young, compassionate with the aged, sympathetic with the striving, and tolerant of the weak and strong. Because someday in your life you will have been all of these."
— George Washington Carver

"Her fever is 100.1. You need to pick her up as soon as possible."

Miss Donna said this in a brisk, deliberate manner without pausing to consider what Janelle's day had been like by 9:30 a.m.

"Yes…yes. I said Marissa needs to be picked up now. We will see you shortly."

Marissa was set down on her back in the crib with her name on it. She was not quite old enough to look up, but in a moment, she saw the face of a new teacher looking down at her. In a moment, she was held close by an adult. This adult felt different from Miss Donna. She didn't have the sense of hurry and briskness that inevitably becomes the manner of every teacher.

Her name was Miss Sarah, but that didn't matter to Marissa, since she was only four months old, and all she cared about was feeling safe. Marissa was not truly sick. Miss Donna was busy and hadn't noticed that Marissa's grandma, who had had custody of Marissa since birth, had simply tucked more blankets around her than necessary that morning.

Janelle was the kindest of grandmas. But she was a grandma about twenty years before she expected to be. Her daughter had become pregnant at fourteen, and the family had decided she was simply too young, so she was not given the chance to be Marissa's mom.

When God's Light Childcare called Janelle that morning, reporting her granddaughter had a fever, it was an inconvenience. She had been in a meeting with an important business partner, but she made no excuses to the daycare staff. Marissa was more important to Janelle than any business partners. Marissa's grandmother simply thanked the new teacher and waved to Miss Donna, who had moved on to catching up with the part-time daycare worker whose job it was to give the other teachers their breaks.

"I think the way we react to things is a big indicator of our character and what type of person we are."
— Zendaya

"We are so sorry, so, so sorry."

She knew these words, for Janelle had heard them before.

This time it wasn't said in Miss Donna's brisk, distracted tone. It was spoken with a broken heart. Mary was genuinely sorry. Mary and her husband owned God's Light Childcare. They knew each family by name and cared deeply for each of them.

It was a Monday in December. I had enjoyed a lovely weekend and been very happy on my way to God's Light Childcare. But when I walked around the corner, I did not see a beautifully painted early learning center. I saw a blackened building surrounded by fire engines with my dear boss wrapped tightly in a heavy, long coat, tears flowing down her face and a line of cars with miserable, confused parents and teachers.

God's Light had a campus, which is unusual for most programs. The building Miss Donna and I worked in was simply called "The Baby's House." It had beautiful landscaping with classroom gardens. The parking lot was even nicely arranged.

The feeling could be described simply as peaceful, but that morning it was anything but.

The Baby's House was smaller and to the side of everything else. It had its own small garden and a beautiful, paved walkway that edged away from everything else. We had a cute, covered area that sheltered our bright-red, six-carriage stroller.

Our building was unmarked by the fire. In fact, if you were only to look at our area of the campus, you would never realize the chaos going on around it.

The police interviewed every staff member that day except me. All day, firefighters, police, and construction workers were at and around the daycare. But aside from all that, something very odd was going on that day.

Juice, coffee, and muffins kept appearing for the staff, clients, police, and investigators. I wondered where it was all coming from, but I was so busy doing my job that I didn't really think too much of it.

We all felt great sadness, and generally, we did not want to be there. Everyone left as soon as they could. No one lingered, no quiet chatting or gossiping was heard. Everyone did their interview and left.

Everyone except for Miss Terri.

Miss Terri had said hello to me briefly when I started working at God's Light Childcare and joked about how challenging being a toddler teacher is. (That was what she did.) She was kind to me and seemed to have a sense of humor that kept her energy up throughout the day.

I started working in the Baby House section of God's Light in winter. Some evenings, I would go to the main center where I would see Miss Terri. She was always hustling around, cleaning up, sanitizing, putting things where they belonged, and making sure everything was nice. She seemed to take a lot of pride in her work, and I liked her for it because I was the same way. My classroom was more important to me than anything; it was the greatest thing I had to take care of after the children.

As it turns out, my assumptions about people are not always accurate and my readiness to accept them isn't always a good thing. I wanted Miss Terri to be a good person, so that is what I saw in her.

Three days after the fire, we found out Miss Terri was an arsonist.

Journal Prompt

1.) Why do you think it is important for a daycare owner knows every family?
2.) How do you think this fire and interruption in services would have been for parents if they did not feel the director knew them?
3.) What thoughts would go through your mind if you found out you were very mistaken about someone like I was about Miss Terri?
4.) Would your sense of belonging be altered by an experience like I had at God's Light Childcare? How would that feeling affect you?
5.) Do you think it would be smart to give teachers a script when they call parents to report fevers, or would that leave parents feeling less like they belong in the program?

Project

Create a script you would use to make the situation better. In my businesses, I have found that automation removes the stress that Miss Donna experienced in this story.

Chapter 12

The Kindness of Miss Rose

"I think when you're young, you're a lot more open-minded, and sometimes you're a lot more perceptive about what's going on in the world."
— Zendaya

"Next time just call me, and I will come wherever you are."

I have written about many moments of kindness thus far in this book, and I will share many more in the following chapters. Some kindnesses were given with ulterior motives, and the person who gave them brought sorrow to my heart that lasted decades, but it was different with Miss Rose.

Twenty-eight years is a long time to serve in the early learning industry, let alone at the same program. When I originally wrote this chapter two months ago, I couldn't remember the name of the first daycare I had worked at full-time (in which I worked with infants under Miss Rose's leadership), but as I researched this book, not only did I remember, but I found the daycare's website and phone number, and I discovered it still has the most wonderful director in the world. Or, at least in my world!

"Next time just call me, and I will come wherever you are," Miss Rose had said. These were the kindest and most welcome words I could have received that freezing December morning, or oddly enough, to this day. They confirmed, at least for a time, that I belonged at Comfort Care Learning Center.

It was so snowy and ever so cold when Miss Rose told me to call her anytime. I took two buses to get to Comfort Care; it wasn't close to my apartment like Weber Street Daycare had been. I made it to the first bus with plenty of time, but then I had to wait fifteen minutes for the next bus.

At the Comfort Care Learning Center, the children, parents, and staff called me Teacher Sarah if Miss Rose was around. When she was not, I was simply invisible, unimportant, and didn't belong. The woman who worked in the other infant room was kind to me in an indifferent sort of way. I think her name was Susan.

Teacher Susan was the most wonderful gossip and made talking with her fun and, when I think about it, I must say, she made me feel included. She had a daughter in high school who would often visit. I was in awe of the energy and happiness she brought wherever she went. As I write this, my own daughter is twelve, and I imagine she would also love to visit an infant room every day after school.

Susan's daughter was not the only one who visited the infant room. Many staff members came in, utterly ignoring me, even though I was actually in charge. But Susan's daughter was so sweet to me and would talk to me about what she was doing at school, where she and her mom were going after work, and on Mondays, what she had done over the weekend.

She was generous by just having kind, animated conversations with whoever was in her proximity at the time. She didn't judge me for my discount store clothes and lack of flare or quiet manner. Susan's daughter just wanted someone to talk to just as Jenna at Weber Daycare had wanted. But, unlike Jenna, Susan's daughter could visit quietly at naptime, and so provided company on days when she didn't have school.

Often, I wish I could go back and hang out with my old self and give pointers, words of encouragement, buy myself a good meal, and gift myself something like maybe a nice set of dishes. But, in this case, I wish I could go back to tell myself to stand up to those teachers and inform them it was my classroom, so they needed to take care of their own students and take their breaks elsewhere.

As it turned out, Miss Rose noticed what was going on and told them to stop coming into my classroom, so they left me alone. At that point, I started to feel a sense of belonging at Comfort Care Learning Center.

Each day, Miss Rose dressed in business attire. She was very slender with long hair that she did in Hollywood curls every day regardless of the weather. Miss Rose was never disrespected or taken lightly because of her kindness. She was a stark contrast to Miss Doris. No one respected Miss Doris; everyone mocked her behind her back. She wore cut-off sweats and a stretched-out, knit button-down shirt with white Velcro shoes every day.

I wonder if Miss Rose found a place of belonging as I believe Miss Doris did. The difference may be that Miss Doris' belonging was based on reaching the highest level she would ever rise to, feeling stuck, and being resigned to never being taken seriously, while Miss Rose felt limitless, empowered, and confident. It is amazing the different forms that belonging takes and what goes into leading a person into their particular state of belonging.

Unlike Brené Brown, author of my favorite book, *Braving the Wilderness*, I am not a social scientist. I am a storyteller and curious daycare teacher who has observed decades of interactions between adults and children from all backgrounds.

One thing I enjoy about hosting my podcast *Stories, Inspirations, and Moving Forward* is I get the chance to listen to even more stories. Maybe one day I will meet Brené Brown and go to one of her speaking events. I absolutely love to surround myself with interesting people.

For now, I am glad to tell people's stories, listen to their stories, and learn. Every day, more and more people become celebrities to me as I realize every person has something remarkable about them.

Truthfully, I wish I could go back to talk to both Miss Rose and Miss Doris. I wonder how old they were back then. When I worked with them, they may have been the age I am now. How quickly time goes by. And by now, I have been formed and further sculpted by the many experiences I had as Sarah Taron.

Life is so fascinating when you simply give yourself a moment to reflect, yet as a young woman, I had hardly a moment to reflect. My life was about surviving with dignity. If I'd had less pride, I think I could have stayed longer in New York and, indeed, in Colorado. Perhaps if I would have taken the financial assistance my oldest brother offered I would have stayed.

Just as I am unsure of Susan's name, so I also am unable to remember the real name of the cook at Comfort Care Learning Center, so I will just call her Donna.

Donna was the sort of woman who was always in her element, truly confident in her job, and didn't take flak from anyone. She knew how much food each classroom ate and was very good about sending enough without wasting food. Years later, I worked as a cook at Rainbow Daycare, so I now have an even higher appreciation for Donna. She also made the time to say hello to all of the teachers, and she delivered each cart of meals herself. All the kids knew her by name and were happy to see her and her cart.

About a week into working at Comfort Care, Donna said, "So, Susan tells me you eat four bowls of cereal every morning from the baby snack cupboard. Don't you have anything to eat at home, girl?"

The truth was no, I didn't have food at home beyond what I could buy from the food liquidation store a block from my house. I would have been mortified to tell anyone else, but Donna didn't make me feel embarrassed. All she did was quietly tell me to stop by the kitchen on my way home that evening—she knew there would be some food left over from that day's lunch. Sure enough, when my shift was over, Donna had set a big portion of food aside for me. Donna fed me every day for the next three months.

Three months later, I had an even smaller apartment closer to Comfort Care. My heating bill dropped because it was spring, so I had more money and was finally able to feed myself. But I will always be grateful to Donna.

To illustrate various points to clients now, I tell stories of past families. Three of those stories come from Comfort Care Learning Center.

The first one is about a little girl named Sarah. I think I remember her so clearly because we have the same name, and her parents happily remarked on that fact more than once. I tell clients about the time when Sarah came down with scarlet fever and her parents tried to bring her to daycare.

Although as I write, we are in the middle of a global pandemic, it seems crazy that a deadly disease, the leading cause of infant mortality in the Victorian era (responsible for 36,000 recorded deaths in the first decade of the twentieth century in England and Wales), could even be brought into a daycare.

The part I emphasize with clients is to communicate with the center and follow daycare policy. Miss Rose dealt with this situation with so much grace that the family did not feel ashamed.

The second story is about a little one I remember so clearly named Gavin. I even remember how immensely proud of him I was the first time he pulled himself up. I excitedly told his mom I had seen him standing up. Rather than her face lighting up with pride, she looked disappointed. After, Susan taught me an important lesson I still follow: Never tell parents you saw their child do something for the first time. To this day, I am grateful to Susan.

And the third story I remember from Comfort Care was of a toddler boy named Love Angel. Believe it or not, I don't tell the story to illustrate that parents choose all sorts of names. I tell it because Love's mom stands out for how beautifully she was always put together. Susan used to joke with me that Love's mom only made us feel dumpy because we were. But I was so impressed that along with everything she put into being a mother, she still took the time to maintain herself. I don't know how she felt in her personal life—whether she dressed up to make herself feel acceptable or whether it was because she celebrated a firm sense of belonging.

As I find myself saying at the end of every chapter, I wonder where each of these children are all these years later. And, I must say, I do miss Susan as I write this. I am truly grateful for her including me in all her gossip, for telling Donna that I was underfed, and for the energy her daughter brought to the infant area of Comfort Care Learning Center.

Journal Prompt

1.) How can you be a Miss Rose in someone's life?

2.) If you are a mother, do you resonate with Love Angel's mom?

3.) Have you had a director who was as wonderful, understanding, and supportive of her teachers as Miss Rose was?

4.) What would you do if a family brought a baby in with scarlet fever? Would you judge them or address them with kindness and compassion like Miss Rose did?

"Love and kindness are never wasted. They always make a difference. They bless the one who receives them, and they bless you, the giver."
— Barbara De Angelis

Project

Create a Pinterest board of a Miss Rose. What would she wear, how would she decorate her office, what would she surround herself with to help her be kind in a job that is so often extremely stressful?

Chapter 13

Brooke and Elizabeth, All But Sisters

"When people show loyalty to you, you take care of those who are with you. It's how it goes with everything. If you have a small circle of friends, and one of those friends doesn't stay loyal to you, they don't stay your friend for very long."
— John Cena

"No, no, no! You go over there, and I will say 'Stop, you go to bed now.'"

"But...no.... We go out shopping and then *you*...."

Brooke and Elizabeth were two friends who made sense and absolutely did not make sense. Every day they played together, even though they rarely agreed on how, where, or what to play. And yet, they were entirely inseparable.

College Way Child Development Center was a popular daycare with a waiting list so long that families paid to get on it. At that time, we didn't have a childcare shortage like we do now in Washington State. College Way Child Development Center was sought after in part because the early learning providers were taught to textbook standards how to do their job to the highest standard.

Their business model was like none I have ever seen. Except for five core teachers, staff could only stay for two years, and the application process was not easy. It was a training school, and they did not employ individuals who were just looking for a paycheck. Everything was perfect: the toys were new, the walls were always clean, the classrooms always seemed to be perfectly arranged (almost staged), and the playground never looked chaotic or out of order.

In my two years there, I never felt stressed or under pressure like I have in other facilities. Every teacher knew what their responsibilities were and that they were supported. College Way certainly had a hierarchy, but it did not allow bullying or belittling—everyone had a role, and beyond the five core teachers, everyone was there to learn, not to take part in decision making or leadership.

Brooke and Elizabeth were above this rigid system, though. Their play simply couldn't be manufactured, and the teachers could not redirect them. We could not frame their play to support the textbook interactions College Way was trying to teach child development staff. (Looking back, I am proud of that fact. True play should be beyond academic control.)

The girls were best friends *and* enemies. They went back and forth so many times the teachers didn't have a chance to resolve anything. Later, I learned children often have the imagination to work out their own conflicts, and sometimes they will even create problems to have something to solve. This fits nicely into my philosophy about the importance of play in learning.

Brooke and Elizabeth's mothers were on staff when I was there, and I heard after two years at the incredible College Way Child Development Center that they started a mini-daycare center together. So, it seems College Way created exactly what it was designed to create. Within two years, Brooke and Elizabeth's moms knew how to run a daycare and thus make more high-quality childcare available. I am always amazed at how well things work when done intentionally.

The way Miss Doris ran her daycare could best be described as spiteful and sloppy. The way Miss Karma of College Way Child Development Center ran things could be described as kindly and intentionally. Miss Karma had her eyes on the future. (And yes, Karma, is her real name.)

Karma was an excellent director, but she did not stay long at College Way. She soon moved on to a specialized program that focused on supporting other childcare programs in readying students for kindergarten.

Brooke and Elizabeth's mothers were both single, and they either weren't caught up in the dating world or they simply had a firm sense of belonging. Brooke and Elizabeth are now in their early twenties, and I wish them the world.

Journal Prompt
1) Have you worked with children who seemed to need behavior management but ended up resolving things before you got to them?
2) What would happen to a child's sense of belonging if you allowed them a moment to work things out before swooping in to save them?

Project

Write a playbook of behavior management issues and responses that are easy fixes so you feel ready if tensions between children seem to escalate. This practice has really given me peace of mind since I know I have a solution in my back pocket just in case. Sometimes knowing I have an awesome playbook gives me the peace of mind not to step in right away if I feel a conflict coming.

Chapter 14

Angel, the Angelic Child Who Did Not Belong

"I don't have to try to be perfect at everything."
— Cindy Crawford

Since I was fourteen, I have always had an affinity for Cindy Crawford because she was my height (five-foot, nine-inches), and she had the confidence I wanted. She was also the mother of twins and, as you know, I am a twin. My mom had an exercise video of Crawford's she made to lose pregnancy weight and return to her marvelous supermodel tone after carrying twins to full term.

When I first wrote this chapter, I had a quote at the beginning that I selected because it followed the theme of not being perfect. But then as I thought about it, I thought it would be better to quote someone I related to. I found Cindy Crawford said it best.

Truly, to make a difference and do well, to contribute, you do not have to be the best at whatever you are doing. Simply being there, showing up, and caring is what matters!

"You need to especially be careful at mealtime because she has three major allergies we know of."

Not only did Angel bring her own box of meals, but she had a portion of the lunch area to herself because we didn't want kids who wanted to share to slip her food that would hurt her. She also had her own batch of Play-Doh the cook had made especially for her. That was only the beginning, but I really do feel that the teachers at College Way Child Development Center did a wonderful job of including Angel and creating a place for her within the community.

Everyone at College Way Child Development Center knew about Angel and the rules she came with. She was beautifully dressed and went about her life in a careful way. She didn't run around the beautifully curated play yard or ask for help putting on a helmet so she could use the tricycles.

She was doted on rather than looked down upon, unlike another little girl named Megan who was vegetarian with a gluten sensitivity. The reason is unfair, and I would like to say I was immune and guiltless in this favoritism. The reason, in fact, had nothing to do with Angel and everything to do with Angel's uncle.

Angel was picked up almost every afternoon by two parents who only had eyes for their beautiful daughter with allergies to so many things. The only staff person they interacted with was the director who personally greeted them and was completely up to date on Angel's day.

Once or twice a month, Angel's uncle, whose name will go unwritten, picked her up. He was tall and handsome, with an impossible tan in all seasons. It didn't matter if he was well dressed or in a hoodie; all the teachers hoped he would talk to them. He remembered everyone's names and what they had said the last time he talked to them.

Though it may be said that a lot had been stacked against Angel, she was happy and her life has probably been much different from that of Morgan whom we talked about in an earlier chapter. Surely, Angel was adored. She was the angel in so many people's worlds. I hope she is doing well. I hope no more medical issues arose as she grew up.

I wonder if Angel found a bit of courage by going to an early learning program that wasn't specialized for children with high sensitivities. Did her parents' anxiety affect her, or did she have the confidence her uncle exhibited on his occasional visits? It absolutely fascinates me how much goes into the making of every child. Sometimes just having that one confident adult around makes all the difference to a child.

Journal Prompt

1) How would you help a child with extreme sensitivities feel included in your classroom?
2) How would you give them a sense of belonging when they had been set apart all their life?

Project

Time yourself on how long it takes to find a Play-Doh recipe free of flour and write out a menu that is gluten, dairy, and nut free. It takes a little bit of time and will make you realize how this caused Angel to be treated differently in the program, even though that was not at all the intention.

Chapter 15

Summer, Daughter of a Determined Teenager

"When you say 'control freak' and 'OCD' and 'organized,' that suggests someone who's cold in nature, and I'm just not. Like, I'm really open when it comes to letting people in. But I just like my house to be neat, and I don't like to make big messes that would hurt people."
— Taylor Swift

Taylor Swift has always fascinated me. I love her work, the voice and message she puts out into the world, and especially this quote because the whole "messy house" issue speaks to me on many levels.

When Swift's song "Love Story" came out, it was all my oldest niece listened to. The song had so much meaning, so many layers, and Swift's music is absolutely gripping.

As I write this book and work through my story, I take frequent breaks to listen to the huge range of music Swift has released. I put a Taylor Swift quote in this chapter because she speaks so often about doing things despite the odds. Even when it seems things are stacked against you, there is still a way to defy the odds. And the mom I tell about in this story was the essence of what Taylor Swift advocates for.

The mom in this chapter had twin girls at seventeen. She was beyond determined to be the incredible mom they needed her to be.

"They can be hard to tell apart. The easiest way to tell them apart is that their mom always puts Summer in yellow."

I got to be Teacher Sarah at The Baby's House in 2007. The Baby's House was a daycare that specialized in babies. It had classes on breastfeeding, bottle feeding, attachment, support groups, and endless answers to frequently asked questions. Someday I would like to offer a daycare with the extensive support, education, and high-quality care that The Baby's House offered to the Colorado Springs community.

Truthfully, I do not remember Summer's sister's name. When I try to remember, I think it is Autumn, but I don't know why I think that. I do remember that my co-teacher always joked about it, saying, "Well, who knows…? She is a teen mom after all." I thought that was such a cruel thing to say, and it is part of why I have such a heart for teen moms everywhere.

To this day, I still think about Summer and Autumn's mommy. She never let anyone help her unpack the babies every morning. She carried them in their car seats, one in each arm, and carefully took them out and handed them over to a teacher.

The twins' mom would come every afternoon to nurse the girls. She often chatted about her life and declared she would never date again. I was twenty at the time, and it absolutely blew my mind that a seventeen-year-old could have twins and do everything she was doing. She was finishing high school online and working during the day. I can't remember where she worked, just how proud she said she was to work there because almost every other place required their workers to be over eighteen.

The twins' mom was remarkable in my mind. She had places to go, people to meet, and she was indeed searching for that sense of belonging, but not in a desperate way. She was in it for her girls, not really to show the world as you would think.

Routine was important to the twins' mom. She dropped the girls off at the same time every day in the same way each time. She got both girls out of the vehicle in their car seats, propped the door open, and brought them in at the same time. She carefully stepped over the low baby gate (which just about gave Miss Donna a heart attack every day), and took each girl out carefully, saying something special to each.

The twins' mom was always friendly with the teachers, and I remember how calm she was in the morning. Later, I learned it was because she gave herself an extra half hour every morning so she was never dashing to work.

I don't know where she worked. The point for her was that she had employment. I remember it being very important to her that she accept as little state assistance as possible.

Many teen moms drop out of school. The twins' mom left school, but rather than dropping out, she enrolled in an online high school. She often talked about how once she finished, she would enroll in online college.

Autumn and Summer's mommy had life figured out better than many adults I have known over the years. She was completely dedicated to her two little girls, and I admire and remember her for that.

I have worked with many young moms, but she stands out the most because she filled the role with such dignity.

> "Anytime someone tells me that I can't do something, I want to do it more."
> — Taylor Swift

Journal Prompt

1.) How do you feel when working with teen parents?

2.) Is it empowering to see a teen parent's determination to defy all expectations, or do you feel pity or compassion? I have found it to be incredibly powerful to notice your feelings rather than judge them.

3.) Do you think childcare programs should put more effort and thought into how they serve teen parents?

Project

Put yourself in the shoes of a teen parent struggling under negative expectations. Think of a way to bolster your mental health. Develop a mantra, and repeat it to yourself in the mirror every morning for a week. Notice the difference it makes for you and then multiply that ninety gazillion times.

Chapter 16

Choosing Another Story, the Decision that Changed Everything

"One of the most beautiful qualities of true friendship is to understand and to be understood."

— Lucius Annaeus Seneca

My dad raised my siblings and me in a world of rights and wrongs. The idea of there being an area or zone outside of or between those simply did not exist. Something was either allowed or not.

Now at the age of thirty-seven, I have had the opportunity to get to know my dad as an adult. And I have realized that he does not see the world in such a structured way. He is generous, kind, and understanding while still being highly principled and consistent. He lives life with more purpose than I have seen in anyone my whole life. While I respect it so much, I have never achieved it or been able to live as he has. I have broken his standards many times.

An idea I was raised with was that men and women can never be friends. The idea is that there is always a sexual intent on one side or the other. In this book, I hoped to tell of such a relationship. I hoped to tell of self-less friendship that didn't involve a crush, but looking back, I can't say it was that entirely.

His name is Tristan, and he was the dear friend to me that I needed so much in that year I was in Colorado Springs.

Our story is not very satisfactory to the outside world, but within my day-to-day survival mentality of moving through life, Tristan was vital. I could not remove him from my story because I would not be who I am today were it not for his friendship. If more people had a friend who was simply available to sit and listen, perhaps they would have more peace in their hearts. Sometimes, I wish I had stayed in the Springs, stayed his friend. But Tristan was ready to get married. He was ten years older than me; he was further along in life than me. And I missed home; I missed being a part of my family's life. Two of my siblings were in serious relationships with wonderful individuals I had never met and another was finishing high school.

I so clearly remember telling Tristan that I was moving home. At first, he didn't say anything; he looked at me a little bit sadly, smiled, and asked if I would like some tea. Looking back, I am glad he didn't say anything right away. It was as though he understood I needed to take another path. He also knew tea was so calming to me and that it was the friendship of understanding I needed.

We never had sex, and I never even slept under the same roof as him. The only time he came to my little apartment, which smelt of bad food and cigarette smoke from my neighbors, was to help me move in. Tristan knew I did not like my apartment, so he had me over at least once a week for a home-cooked meal at his house. Our friendship did not have the climax and culmination that a Hollywood prediction would give it.

Aside from a short phone call to check that I had arrived safely at my parents, I didn't hear from Tristan directly for many, many years. I heard from a mutual friend that he had married and was happy, and that he had sold the business he was working on that we had talked about often.

Our story isn't of heartbreak in the way you would expect. He didn't break my heart with cruelty, unkind words, or putting me down. It is of heartbreak because I chose to move past our friendship because we were looking for different things in life.

So when people share their stories of heartbreak, I do listen with an understanding. I understand leaving someone who is dear. I understand the missed connection. I understand moving forward in life without someone who is so completely loved.

I understand.

I understand.

Journal Prompt

1.) Do you live a life of rights and wrongs, having a firm understanding of how the world operates?

2.) Have you ever had a deep friendship with someone of the opposite sex?

Project

Take time to write a letter to your past self, thanking yourself for making the tough decision to maintain your integrity and follow what you thought then was your path.

Chapter 17

Deciding to Continue, Choosing Belonging

"No matter what happens, be good to people. Being good to people is a wonderful legacy to leave behind."
— Taylor Swift

In April 2008, I met a young man on a blind date. I found belonging with him, a friendship so close to what I had with Tristan. Both men are very distinct from each other, each strong and weak in their own way. The biggest difference is I met Justin when I was ready to get married. I don't believe in soul mates; I believe in timing. For me, the concept of timing is larger than fate; it has power to it and the wonderful sense of mystery that my dad says simply is not meant to be understood.

"And so, journal, today I married him."

That is my favorite line to have written in a lifetime of writing. It was what I wrote in my journal right after marrying my husband.

I married Justin on a rainy September Saturday. I chose that story, and I am honored to be married to him today. We have been through so much in the years since I sat down for that blind date. We have said and done many unkind things to each other, and we have promised to give second chances many times over. And, by now, we are finally dear friends. Now, after all this time, I truly believe there is no hurdle that life can bring that we are not able to overcome.

I find so much power in choosing. My husband has told me many times that making a choice is hard because, in doing so, you are saying "no" to every other option.

On that cold day in Colorado, I chose to leave a love that I was not ready for. I did not know where I was headed except that I knew that place was one move closer to finding a sense of belonging.

My "goodbye" to Tristan was not long or dramatic, it was simply an understanding that I needed to go. It was a conversation over two mugs of hot tea. We didn't talk about me leaving. We talked about Tristan's business that was finally becoming a reality. And we talked about my day at daycare. We didn't talk about the future because we knew it wouldn't include each other.

Journal Prompt

1.) What is a gesture someone has made toward you that made you feel so entirely loved the way I did when Tristan offered me a mug of tea? This was definitely a moment that could have been so painful, but he made it kind.

Project

Find a way to show selfless friendship to someone in your life with no agenda. Even a small motion can make all the difference for someone. I have learned this in my personal life, but even more so with my daycare clients who have gone through life largely unseen and without kindness.

Chapter 18

Rachelle, the Little Girl Who Got Hurt

"The most beautiful people we have known are those who have known defeat, known suffering, known struggle, known loss, and have found their way out of those depths."
— Elisabeth Kübler-Ross

"Me mommy hurt me eye, Mrs. Sarah."

"Your children are not your children. They are the sons and daughters of Life's longing for itself."
— Kahlil Gibran

My heart has been broken many times. But it aches the most when I see a child intentionally hurt by a caregiver. That is multiplied when the perpetrator is the mother. So much must be going on in a mother for her to injure her child. As a mother, I know the depths of feelings that come with parenting.

We mothers face so many pressures and expectations put upon us by society and by sources meant to build us up. We even carry around our very own brand of judgmental baggage. Sometimes all of that is compounded by unseen abuse and sadness. I have been driven by guilt in my own life, which lends me to understand my clients even more clearly.

Rachelle had been in my care for seven months when she started crying with all her soul on that cold September morning. She was sitting on our old, blue couch with a blanket over her lap in my front room. The stove in the corner had heated the room to a perfect temperature, and everything was ready for a wonderful day when she arrived.

Rachelle had been in her mother's custody off and on throughout her life. The system traditionally favors mothers in custody cases. That is changing due to the growing awareness of stories like Rachelle's. Society assumes that violence is inflicted by men, but that just isn't always the case.

Rachelle's mom was a tough woman with a lot of hurt, fear, and anger, and she had felt a sense of belonging for only brief moments throughout her life. She did not trust easily or often, but she did trust me. She had more than one assault on her record, but she was always kind to me. If she felt that anyone was intimidating me or showing disrespect, she would stand up for me.

I hope you especially remember this chapter. It may be the most important and transformational; indeed, I think the situation it describes has kept me within the childcare community.

Every morning was different for Rachelle. School was a place where she felt a burden lifted off of her young self. She had an older quality about her. She was more wary and had a sense of tiredness no naptime could fix.

Sometimes, Rachelle came to my little in-home daycare very upset and exhausted. Sometimes, she would be crying. Sometimes, she would be screaming. Her mom always said, "Love you, Rachelle," right before closing the door, and Rachelle always mimicked it back to her in the tone it was said. Sometimes she was shoved through the door with a "Git in there" and a push on her shoulder, but every time, still, she said, "I love you."

Every story has so many sides, and each person has so many dimensions. We all have so many reasons behind each moment and each and every tone.

Upon arrival, Rachelle didn't want a hug or to interact at all for several minutes. I always had the same blanket folded in a square on the couch and a book within reach for her. I respected her space because I knew it was not afforded to her at home. Perhaps even today, I hesitate to say how much I could and do relate to Rachelle. I understand not being given space to simply feel my own feelings. It is hard when you are rarely given a moment, and then, when it is given, to have that peace taken away.

On that morning, though, Rachelle did not take time for herself. After saying "love you" back to her mother, she held her breath, and as soon as she closed the car door, Rachelle started saying over and over, "Her hurt my eye, Mrs. Sarah. Her hurt my eye."

The first class I took on child protection was way back in 2004, but I remember it clearly. The first thing they teach you is to call Social Services the moment you see a sign of abuse. Do not even take time to understand or judge what happened—simply notify the authorities.

What happened after Rachelle told me about her eye was a whirlwind. The Department of Youth and Family Services told me to call the police right away. The police arrived within minutes and took pictures of Rachelle's eye. About an hour later, social workers arrived and then two more social workers came.

Everyone wanted to take pictures and ask questions. Each time Rachelle said the same thing, and my heart broke over and over.

Rachelle's mommy went to jail that day.

One year later, Rachelle was once again in her mother's custody. Her eye had healed, and Joy continued to say, "I love you," to her.

Even though Joy knew I had called Social Services and the police, she insisted Rachelle stay at my daycare even while Rachelle was in foster care in another area. Joy trusted me, and I know that my making that call got her and Rachelle the help they needed.

By now, Rachelle is starting middle school, and while I am not connected with Joy on social media, I like to think she is a proud and confident mother who has found belonging and knows the power of having confidence in herself as a person.

Eventually, Rachelle left my little daycare as many little ones had done before her. Daycare workers have their hearts broken in many ways, but they have as many ways to heal.

Rachelle certainly was part of the making of me. Wherever she is now, all these years later, as this book is read and passed from hand to hand, I hope Rachelle knows she was loved, treasured, and protected when she was with me at Gooseberry Childcare.

My greatest hope is that she found a similar place of belonging like she did and always will with me in my small A-frame house on a narrow road on the Lummi Indian Reservation. This is my hope for you as well. May you find peace where there was once brokenness.

At this point, peace is really what I wish for most in the world. It is not acclaim, power, or even health that is most important—it is peace.

Journal Prompt

1.) Do you see yourself in Rachelle's story?
2.) If Rachelle were in your classroom, how would you treat her and relate to her as she healed from her horrible assault?
3.) How would you treat her mother after she served her time?
4.) How would you feel if you were given the respect Rachelle's mom gave me?

5.) Would you love and open your heart to Rachelle's mom like I did?

Project

Build or set up a safe place in your home or classroom for children to sit and feel calm and at peace like sweet Rachelle used to every morning. It is absolutely incredible to see the change that comes over children when they have a safe place they can choose to go to. Think about your favorite chair to read in or the blanket you curl up under to watch TV. Kids feel the same way, if not more so.

Chapter 19

Brooke, Showing Kindness to a Teacher Who Did Not Belong

"With all of the bad things that are happening in the world right now, I think we need a message of togetherness and true unity. I believe that starts with personal reflection and then we can find kindness toward each other."
— Marielle Heller

"Come down the slide with me, Teacher; it is so fun!"

When I worked at the College Way Child Development Center, I was told in a hard tone that good teachers never played with one child. We were taught the role of an early learning provider was to facilitate play and to supervise, not to directly play with the children. One main reason I didn't use the real name of that daycare is because that belief is so contrary to my own that it gives me the shivers.

One thing I really disliked about working for other daycares was often feeling like an excluded outsider. I don't know why I was so rarely accepted, but sweet Brooke gave me the feeling of belonging that I had been without before I was her teacher.

Brooke was determined to include me in her play. Her energy was endless, but her kind words and will to include were infectious and continuing. I met Brooke at a time when I was starting to feel more secure and confident. But I still felt the longing I have always felt. My only respite was conversation, sharing of stories, and time spent with others. And that was exactly what Brooke was all about!

"You can hold my hand and be my friend today."

Over my twenty-one years as a childcare provider, I have heard that line said countless times. Brooke didn't say this to children only. She said it daily to teachers as well. And on the days when you were not her favorite, she certainly didn't shun you. However, her mother was not this way. She was unkind to me. She didn't directly shun me; she showed her dislike by not supporting me when I needed help or advice.

Miss Melissa was unkind. Indeed, she was Brooke's mother. Usually, I do not speak as blatantly as other teachers do, but in this case I must. It was as if she had a burr up her butt. Miss Melissa went about her day as though she were better—better educated, more informed, more knowledgeable—than the rest of us. She was so much better, except she didn't share her knowledge as our director wanted. If anyone did something she didn't think was up to standard, she wrote it down and brought it to the director.

In writing this book, for the first time I can look back on her with kindness and concern. Was Miss Melissa suffering because she felt left out? Was she in the depths of feeling a lack of belonging? Did her unkindness come from someone else's cruelty? Was she in a relationship that was breaking her heart and body? Now that I think about it, she always wore long sleeves and didn't want to go home. Was this why Brooke followed every rule so closely and showed so much kindness and compassion?

It may be that lack of belonging affects everyone differently. And that possibility now makes me see Brooke and Miss Melissa in another light.

Journal Prompt

1.) Has there been a time when you did not feel you belonged in your own classroom?
2.) Have you felt entirely broken until the children, in their quiet kindness, brought you the healing and strength you needed?

Project

One of my favorite thoughts is to be kind to the unkind because they need it the most. Next time you are treated thoughtlessly, take a moment to be curious about the other person. I wonder how I would have reacted if I had noticed Miss

Melissa's sleeves or given her the benefit of the doubt.

Chapter 20

The Girl Who Decided Being Different Was Okay

"Life is wherever you are at. Whatever you are doing is enough. You don't need to do everything well all of the time. When you live like that, it is a huge relief."
— Cindy Crawford

"Sticking with your vision is so important."
— Zendaya

The idea of starting a new chapter in your life is so prevalent, and whenever we do, it is often acknowledged and celebrated.

This chapter is a bit of a transition in this book because it starts telling a bit more about my making, my personal story. When I told my twin sister about this book and asked her permission to use her given, legal name, she said no, and that I didn't need it anyway because I was just writing a book about my childcare career.

I want you to understand that being a childcare provider is more than what happens in the classroom. So much goes into what happens in the classroom, and that is why it is important to share my whole story.

I hope this chapter will speak to you because, at some point, we really do need to realize it is okay to be different. And regardless of your vocation or calling, I want you to see you are more than that one thing. You are so multi-facilitated!

Once we stop trying to be like everyone else, we become unique people who can truly make a difference in the world. And perhaps that different, unique person can play a part in bringing peace and creativity to the world.

This second part of *The Making of Mia* is all about life's chapters and the process of deciding. In this case, choosing to be different is a freeing experience. In the following chapters, I refer to myself in the third person a couple of times. The reason is simple—it will help you see yourself in my story because, indeed, I truly am coming to understand that we all have more in common than the world allows us to see. Referring to myself as an outsider, in third person, gives me a unique feeling of objectivity that I didn't have back then. I was living from moment-to-moment and couldn't really understand the gravity of my experiences.

Books and podcasts about living a more fulfilled life advocate for living moment to moment. Supposedly, doing so leads to heightened appreciation. But when I was living with heightened awareness back when I was broke, I felt one misstep would send me into the abyss of homelessness.

It seems like people are not allowed to see themselves as they are or tell their stories. That is why I have chosen to write this book and host a podcast about sharing stories.

I also decided to stop pressuring myself to be the perfect teacher, changing from program to program. I decided I wanted to live with integrity. Once I decided to stop trying to anticipate what everyone else would think and expect, I found peace and belonging. And truly, it didn't take leaving Colorado or New York or anywhere for that to happen. It wasn't anyone's fault; it was a part of the process.

Choosing to be perfectly yourself, allowing yourself to grow for yourself, makes the difference. After just one year of intentionally working on myself and my business and asking myself the hard why questions, I hardly recognize myself. Growth happens incredibly fast when you finally start doing it for yourself.

Families are blessed more when their members simply let go of the need to be perfect. If this message reaches just one person, all that has gone into writing this book will be worth it!

Decide today to be different. Decide today to be perfectly yourself. Decide today to stop trying to be someone else.

Journal Prompt

1.) Realizing it is okay to be different is so powerful. When I worked for other daycare programs, I never truly belonged because I was not normal. I desired to serve families and be professional in a way that just wasn't attractive to other workers. I wasn't better, I was simply different, with a bigger goal.
2.) When and/or how do you feel out of place?
3.) What does it takes to realize it is okay to be different, and is that something you need in order to grow?
4.) What do you think would happen if everyone allowed themselves to become a little bit different?

Project

Create a Pinterest board of what your "authentic self is" with a completely accepting and non-judgmental mindset. As you look over the finished product, notice that you may not be normal. And then find someone to give you a high-five on my behalf. Once people are able to see themselves as themselves, I think there will be more fulfilment in the world.

Chapter 21

Finding Your Safe Place

"The ache for home lives in all of us, the safe place where we can go as we are and not be questioned."
— Maya Angelou

Everyone needs a safe place. Everyone talks about having a comfort zone. In fact, we even designate a whole category of food as dedicated to comfort!

Self-help literature is a whole section of the library and every bookstore. The reason this book is not in the self-help section is it is not about helping yourself—it is about the world, the preschool classroom, and especially parenthood.

"The comfort zone is where good ideas go to die."

This quote is from one of my favorite mentors, and it really is true. But when I was nineteen, I was so far from a feeling of belonging that I wished I had a safe place. Take a moment to think of some really small things that make you feel safe. Where do you go when you feel bitterly disappointed, but don't want anyone to see that you feel that way?

When I left home in 2004, I had two pieces of carry-on luggage and a lot of memories and experiences. The only safe place I brought with me was my journal. That was where I went when I felt sad, scared, or just needed somewhere to be myself. I wrote and wrote and wrote. My Bible was also in my luggage, and it, too, was a dear friend.

I encourage you to find one thing. And as you move through life and expand yourself to reach your goals and grow, please don't entirely lose touch with your safe place. You need somewhere to go where you can be entirely yourself.

As Zendaya, one of my favorite actresses, says, *home* is wherever you are, not a location but a way of being. I wish I had understood that a long time ago. But really...if I had, there would be no story.

Journal Prompt

    1.) Where and/or what is your comfort zone?

    2.) Do you think it is okay to stay in that safe place?

Project

Create a safe place in your home like I created for myself as I moved around. My safe place was where I had my spiritual practice and wrote. Note the huge difference between a safe place and your comfort zone. I fully agree with my mentor when she says that your comfort zone is where dreams go to die. I don't want your dreams to die. I want you to grow into the amazing human you are designed to be, but I want you to take your safe place with you as I have.

Chapter 22

Adult Conversations, Changing the Way We Interact

"It isn't what we say or think that defines us, but what we do."
— Jane Austen

July 2009 was my last month working in someone else's daycare. Looking back, it astounds me that so much happened within five years. During the years I spent working for other people, I poured more into my job than I should have. But those jobs were all I had—they were the most important things. It seems like in just a breath, twelve years went by. Twelve years have passed since our little home was licensed to provide childcare. How drastically my ideas have changed.

One principle has always stayed the same: the most important, lasting learning happens through play. The best early learning comes from the play yard and interactions in the classroom, not directly from a teacher.

Adult conversation is the real difference between daycare centers and in-home daycare. In the latter, you have no co-teachers, no one to share lunch with, no one to gossip with, no one to sit with on a bench when you are supposed to be moving around the play yard. But when I worked in a daycare center with other teachers, I felt the most lonely and disconnected I have ever felt.

For some reason, I was never really liked, so I hid behind and was so fascinated by the Mias of the classrooms. It was really the Rachelles and Marissas I was there for. The little ones who were seen but unseen.

The power of being known is so huge and so powerful. Yes, everyone has different needs, and that somehow needs to be honored in daycare. Adult conversation is important, but so are the haughty conversations that Mia and her friends had. They are what makes becoming and making possible.

"I put my heart and soul into my work and have lost my mind in the process."
— Vincent Van Gogh

Journal Prompt

1) What does adult conversation mean to you?
2) Is it important to have other adults to talk to, or would you rather have a program all by yourself and interact only with the children?

Project

Adult conversation can go in so many directions. For this chapter's project, make a list of people you can reach out to when you need to talk things out. For me, this list includes directors, coaches, siblings, and friends. I have their names and numbers, and sometimes that alone brings me comfort. Whether we call ourselves introverts or extroverts, we all need connection, and it is so helpful to know you have someone to reach out to.

Chapter 23

Where Broken Hearts Go

"Everything I've done has had purpose and has been passionate and has been executed in the best way that I knew how. Maybe that's not the perfect way. Maybe that's not the easiest way. But it's the best way I knew how to do it."
— Julia Roberts

Broken hearts can be found in so many places, but you would not think the preschool classroom would be among them. But that is the truth. In the preschool classroom, many teachers are not earning enough money to make rent. The classrooms are full of children from broken homes.

I told a dear friend of mine that the benefit of working at a daycare is you are expected to always be happy, so you are. The expectation of always smiling and being chipper makes it easier to create the facade of being happy, so it becomes a beautiful and reliable mask.

Typically, when people apply for jobs in early learning, it is not because they feel a lifelong call to walk with children as they experience the most precious phases, the ones that shape whom they will be as adults. However, some bright and shiny personalities do work in early learning, and many of them become public speakers, authors, and gurus who speak of the magic and importance of an often-overlooked industry.

I don't necessarily want to be a guru. I want to be an author who speaks truth about the sadness, emptiness, and lack of direction in the hearts and minds of the team members of various programs. They are never far from my thoughts and heart, and I bear their burdens now as I write this book.

The childcare industry is full of broken hearts.

When I started this book, I surely didn't mean to include a chapter about broken hearts. But, dear reader, the purpose of this book is to give you real perspective on the early learning world.

Magazines and blogs usually have beautiful, bright, crisp images of children playing joyfully. Every child has clean, vibrant, and fresh clothing; matching shoes; and hair free of lice. This is partly why deciding on a cover for *The Making of Mia* was such a struggle. The cover I liked best was a little girl walking in a beautiful wheat field, looking up dreamily into a fantastic blue sky. She had the long perfect curls I describe at the beginning of the book. While the image was compelling to me, it did not feel quite right. And so, I chose the picture you now see: a little girl of African descent standing on her head, with a beautiful smile of triumph. This little girl is not Mia, or really any of the little girls I've taught. She is the child one of my favorite celebrities, Zendaya, is there to inspire.

Zendaya speaks loudly about racial issues, but also about the need to see people as they are, to find home where you are, and to rise above the petty. I chose a cover that has the feeling of life, growth, and joy, but also of so much more to come.

I want the world to understand the childcare industry as more than babysitting, but not as an academic pursuit either. I guess people have not known how to let early learning providers into the larger conversation of bringing world peace. And that is what I want this book to bring daycare workers closer to.

We hold the hearts, minds, and moments that are so dear, so precious, and truthfully, the future of the nations. We are on the outside, left out of the conversation on mental health, the economy, social media, politics, yet everything affects us.

Truthfully, there are many broken hearts at daycare. And that is not true only for the students. Teachers also seek a feeling of belonging they have a hard time finding, and many barely hold on to self-respect because they go home to empty apartments and bills they can't pay.

The daycare I most clearly remember is Weber Street Daycare—the daycare Miss Doris directed and where I met the beautiful four-year-old this book is named for. When I found a photograph of this daycare while researching this book, my heart sank. So many memories came back. I saw my twenty-one-year-old frame walking through the chain-link gate each morning, and felt the cold metal on my hand. I heard the heavy clink of the latch falling back into place. I clearly remembered my trepidation and the desperate feeling of hope I slid over that feeling.

And then I remembered glancing through the large window at Miss Doris' empty desk (she was always late to work), allowing a light sigh of relief out before opening the front door. That was how every morning began. I carried a canvas shoulder bag with me everywhere. It had my wallet, flip phone, books (one for myself and several for the kids), and my trusty water bottle.

When I looked at the picture of Weber Street Daycare on Google, I was surprised by how small it was. I don't remember it being so small. I wanted to call around to find out how many children the daycare had been licensed for and why it was listed as permanently closed. But then I remembered my purpose is to write my story and Mia's story and talk about finding our sense of belonging.

The teachers all knew Mia by the tone of her voice, the flip of her curly ponytail. I remember the toddler teacher saying Mia had always had a spark of energy and sass. The toddler teacher spoke of this with great pride, and then laughing as she got to see others trying to work with Mia's boundless energy.

I really liked that toddler teacher. She had the same way of gossiping as Susan from Comfort Care in New York, except her flavor included a glimmer of being all-knowing, just a bit smarter. And, of course, I'd kind of like to meet her again. She was a good person and a fun teacher in her own right.

Mia never walked alone. When she strutted around the play yard, it was always with her arms linked with two other girls, walking confidently. While happy and full of energy, she was continually telling others they were not her friend anymore for this or that reason. In my memory of those six months, I don't recall any of the children trying to challenge or question her declarations of discontinued friendship. It was simply as Mia said it was. Whenever she decided it was their turn to be her friend again, they were happy about it.

> "You may give them your love but not your thoughts,
> For they have their own thoughts.
> You may house their bodies but not their souls,
> For their souls dwell in the house of tomorrow, which you cannot visit, not even in your dreams.
> You may strive to be like them, but seek not to make them like you.
> For life goes not backward nor tarries with yesterday."
> — Kahlil Gibran

Even if the center director doesn't care, like Miss Doris didn't care, about what goes on or how professional the daycare center is, as a teacher, you kind of feel you should jump in whenever you even feel a conflict coming on. Perhaps Miss Doris' not caring came from years and years of caring until something happened that made her say, "To heck with it all." Was she once a creative teacher who brought library books to early learners?

In Mia's case, it just wasn't worth stepping in because the other children truly did not seem too troubled when she exiled them from her friend circle. It was as if they were almost glad to have been her friend even for a little while. And so, she was more of a force of nature than anything. The kids (and teachers, really) accepted that she would do as she would do. She was confident in herself, and it appeared she had no lack of belonging.

I started this book by asking what lesson you would share with the world as your legacy, something your kids and the world could know about you. Creating a legacy is really what *The Making of Mia* is for me. I asked what resolve and wish you would give, and I really encourage you to dig into that and think about what it is because your answer matters. Whether you think so or not, you are important and loved.

I wish for peace in the hearts of people everywhere. I suffered a lot working in a field that hardly paid minimum wage. But those troubles and struggles brought me to where I am now, and I hope I will never forget that. And that is why I needed to write it down. I do not wish for everyone to be given a certain amount of money or success—rather I wish them peace, confidence, and the knowledge that they are loved.

So many families of all different economic statuses suffer from feeling unseen. Sometimes, I am the first to ask what they want out of life, and I am a daycare worker. How different the world would be if your legacy were simply a message of love and support. That doesn't sound like a lot, but it is needed.

I plan to go back to Colorado again. I plan to go to my old church, to stay with my dear aunt, to visit God's Light Learning Center, to visit the homes of old friends, and to meet up with people I cared for and haven't seen for decades. A part of me wants to go alone, like a selfcare retreat, almost, to feel the loneliness I felt before. But another part of me wants to triumphantly bring my husband and children.

Time really is an odd thing; it is really the only consistent thing in the world. And yet, we are always amazed at how it passes.

As I wrote this book, I did a simple search for Tristan by reaching out to a mutual friend. He had left Colorado Springs, selling his little house and his business months after I moved back to Washington. He was still married happily and had seven children. He was recovering from COVID, and while I felt concern for him, I had the feeling he would be better soon. And so I am at peace and happy for him as I always knew I would be.

I have chosen to share my story. I decided that the world needs to know how I lived, loved, and what drives me forward to continue working in the wonderful world of early learning. I have known dear friendship as well as some disappointments, but I truly am blessed.

Yes, broken hearts do come here. But I do not believe those hearts need to stay broken. In these chapters, you will read of healing and hope. We all have the same problem: We all need to be seen. We all need to be heard. We all need to be saved from loneliness. But I have come to realize that healing really comes when we realize it can't come from outside of ourselves.

Without writing this story, my work and I would simply slip away into nothingness. If you had not picked up this book, you would never have the unique pleasure of meeting Mia, Morgan, Jenna, Julia, Alice, Summer, Brooke, Maliki, Rachelle, Masina, and the contrasting characters who make a special point.

The name Tristan came to me in a dream, and I am 100 percent content with it. It is close to his real name, and I hope he finds himself in this book. I like to imagine the pride he might feel to see that I have grown and continued to pursue my dream of bringing peace to a world where sadness exists.

My younger sister whom you have known as "Eve Grace" is a published author, which is why she chose that pseudonym. I have such high respect for her and for all she has already contributed to the world.

Even though he is only mentioned once, I have even given my intended husband from when I lived at home a false name. He married months after I discontinued our relationship, and I am sure he is a good man.

All the daycare names have been changed, but I have given them names I believe capture their essence. I contrast between two daycares often: Weber Street Daycare and Comfort Care Early Learning. They are both in Colorado Springs, and one day I would like to meet the owners and simply thank them for the difference they made in my life and the catalyst they provided me in continuing in the early learning field. The book has contrasts between two directors (Doris and Miss Rose) and two men who captured my heart (Justin and Tristan).

My dear husband and three biological children are named even though my original plan was not to include them because I wanted this book to be exclusively about daycare. But the more I wrote, the more I realized I simply cannot be taken out of daycare, that my husband and children (Claire, Helen, and Richard) are as much a part of me as Mia and all the children I have served and serve now.

As I originally intended, though, the story is about Sarah Taron, a young woman with a passion for children who is fighting to find a place to belong. But I have seen that she is me and I am her! Sarah Taron fell in love with her best friend, chose another chapter, and another man came into her life and heart and so, she became Sarah Ayers. This is not the end of my story; it is only the beginning. It is so thrilling to think how my life will change once I publish this book and in the many years to come!

Journal Prompt

1. Not everyone sees the preschool classroom as I have. Is there somewhere you feel broken hearts go that other people don't think of?
2. What could you do to acknowledge feelings more within the childcare setting?
3. Do you think it is important for teachers and parents to seek to be in a place of peace as well as to create that for the children they care for?

Project

Throughout this book, I mention what I would have said to my younger self or done for her. Take a moment to remember yourself even ten years ago and think of what you might do for yourself. How did you feel back then, and do you now see a place where broken hearts went? The project in this chapter, really, is just to reflect. I have found so much power in reflection.

Chapter 24

When You Decide to Start Another Chapter

"Goodness is about character—integrity, honesty, kindness, generosity, moral courage, and the like. More than anything else, it is about how we treat other people."
— Dennis Prager

When it comes to personal relationships, some believe we don't choose to move on, to start a new chapter. I have come to believe we do have the power to change our relationships—to close one chapter and create another. Indeed, that is what this chapter is about. I have been married for thirteen years now. And I chose this chapter. I chose to get married.

With each chapter, I have thought about the outcome I wanted. I thought about how I wanted each story, the story of each of these children, to alter the world. I thought about how I wanted to touch the lives of each person who reads my book.

Rather than having a separate answer or lesson come from the individual chapters, I decided I wanted the whole book to speak further and further to one point: learning and belonging come and are most lasting when children are allowed to learn through play.

But this chapter is not directly about children. It is not for you because you relate to the story of a child. No, this chapter is written directly for you, to you, because you are valuable and what happened in my life is needed and of use.

This chapter is about starting new chapters.

This chapter is about a man and a woman, about friendship without intentions aside from being there for each other. Nothing exciting happened, but for me, it was everything. I wasn't his girl and he wasn't my man in the way movies are written, but we were whom we needed to be when we needed to be.

He was kind and safe, a listening and caring ear, and that is what I hope I was for him. I would like to see that memory of a man again, to say thank you for that friendship, but we have simply continued on with life and are in different places as, indeed, I thought we would be.

My desire was the same as all those years ago in Colorado. I wanted to inspire women and families all over the world. I want my message to be strong—there is something better; there is hope beyond your current situation, and you are meant for more!

Sometimes, starting a new chapter is not a grand motion that others can see. Sometimes, it happens in a moment; sometimes, over several weeks.

Tristan.

I said earlier that I don't believe in soul mates, that I believe timing is what brings people together. That doesn't sound very romantic at all, but I truly believe it to be consistent through all of the stories of love. There are so many possibilities of true love; you simply marry who is closest when you are ready. Perhaps one day I will write an entire book around this idea, but not today.

His name was and is Justin.

"And, today, journal, I married him."

Those were the best words I have ever written. And they still are. As I write this book, I wonder how life will change and how I and all those around me will evolve.

When I got married, I was entirely and completely in love with my husband Justin. My past disappeared, and the future held nothing aside from Justin and me and whatever the world brought our way.

I am not sure when it happened, but kindness left our marriage at some point. I felt like the only interactions we had were of him squashing, belittling, and entirely dismissing any idea I had. Every time I wanted to celebrate something, it was overshadowed by something I had done improperly.

Every idea I had was stupid and not enough even to be considered or presented to anyone. And then, before I knew it, I stopped trying. I stopped caring, and I started living alone, even though we were both still sleeping in the same bed every night. It was as though we were invisible to each other, indifferent and without meaning.

In January 2020, the coronavirus was all over the news, and by March, the world had closed down. By April, our children's school was officially canceled, which meant I had lost my home daycare. Rather than the pandemic and its consequences drawing us closer together, Justin and I grew further apart. Resentment built up in my heart as it never had before.

At the same time, I started building an online empire, taking classes on growing an online business, and spreading my wings into the cyber world. By June 2020, I had established a nanny service bringing families and nannies together, and by September, I launched my first coaching program.

I was reaching families in a way I never had before. And people were reaching out to me, not only for my online program and nanny service, but also to thank me for the words of encouragement in a scary time.

My heart was still breaking from the unkindness that had somehow snaked into my precious marriage. And I was still trying to fly under Justin's radar. I thought that if he found out about my online business, he would say something mean or cut me down when I was feeling most vulnerable.

At some point, I decided I was tired of assuming I would be hurt. I remembered the friendship I'd had all the way back in 2006, remembered Tristan and the courage he gave me when I had so many reasons not to believe in myself. I decided it was worth being made fun of, and I pushed forward and decided I needed to do more than create a coaching program for young parents—I needed to write a book for parents. I began to understand more and more that I was not the only one who was feeling the way I was.

It is simply choosing that makes the world of a difference. A thought, a change, one choice...well, that is where this book came from!

Most of my life has been lived in the shadows, and I know that is true of almost everyone. That means most of us are unseen, unknown, and untold. We all live lives and deserve to be seen for the beautiful, spectacular creations we are.

Since I decided to share with my husband my new dream for the future of writing *The Making of Mia* and designing an impactful coaching program, he has hesitantly put his support behind me. He has opened his mouth several times to point out the holes in my plans and reasoning, but then he has decided to give me a bit of space to fall on my own. And when I haven't fallen, he has been there with a high-five and a note of encouragement.

Journal Prompt

1.) Why do you think my friendship with Tristan was so powerful that I remember it all of these years later?

2.) Do you have a Tristan in your past? If so, what difference did a consistent friendship with the opposite sex, free of agendas, mean to you?

Project

What is one small change you could make in your life today that would enable you to start another chapter?

Chapter 25

Malachi, the Baby with Two Stories

"There's so much grey to every story—nothing is so black and white."
— Lisa Ling

Regardless of the mother's story or how she happens upon my daycare, whether she is referred, mandated by the court, happened upon my website, or a neighbor recommended me, each mom has a sense of dignity about her.

Perhaps that is what has fascinated me the most over the years. Some women have been so beat down throughout their lives that by the time they become mothers, they have little self-esteem left. But they have pride in knowing they brought a little person into the world…even if that world is full of scarcity and cruelty.

Scarcity isn't always financial; cruelty isn't always physical.

Every child is different in their own way.

Malachi was a little boy who had two stories. You would think this would be true of most foster children, but it was more so of Malachi.

Foster children have one story: Their family wasn't able to take care of them and they are being passed from family to family with no one truly in control of their life experience.

Malachi wasn't like that. He simply had two stories. An unclear one that I learned parts of, but that was very positive, and the other one that his mom kept secret for the three years Malachi was in my program—the one that made her sad. The stories were polar opposites, but both held a bit of sadness.

Every time I welcome a new child into my daycare I feel as much excitement as fear, or I guess, I should say hesitation. Not the type of hesitation that makes you think about quitting something, but the feeling you have before doing something big. That new child could make your days so much better or so much more hard. Whether a sweet child or not, another child joining the program changes the school's entire dynamic.

When little Malachi started in my program, his mom's first question was, "Do you think he is too small?"

Malachi's mom was one of those moms who dresses beautifully regardless of her plans for the day, whether she will be working, cleaning the house, or going to coffee with a friend. I will always remember she carried a purse; believe it or not, that is not normal for toddler moms. Usually, they still carry a diaper bag. She had a huge white purse with a floral print. And her clothing always complemented it, even though the purse never changed.

I remember exactly what Malachi looked like on his first day: blue and white, snap-down, stripey jammies that felt like terry cloth. He had soft, dark, baby-fuzz hair that was already thinning a little on the back of his head. His eyelashes were dark and thick, and his face was the perfect round common with Cesarean births. His mom always carried him wrapped in a brown plush blanket with a Noah's ark print. She was as consistent in everything.

Something I was taught at Miss Rose's Comfort Care Learning Center is that when each and every child arrives, you squat down in front of them, ask how their morning has been, and look for bruising, runny nose, cough, etc. And yes, you look for children being underweight like the little girl we talked about many chapters back.

When I met Malachi, weight was certainly not a concern that came to mind. Of course, many mothers of infants worry about size, weight, and coloring. They worry over how often their children poop and how they do this or the other. Malachi's mom was concerned about his size, but she did not notice how loose his ligaments were. Every day I assured Malachi's mom that he was indeed the right size, but that if she had any concerns, she should talk to his pediatrician. I have told so many moms this that I now do it without pause.

My job is to take care of little ones, but I am not a medical professional. This is exactly what I have talked about in earlier chapters regarding Child Protective Services. My job is not to investigate bruises where bruises aren't usually, burns where burns wouldn't naturally occur, fears of things other kids don't notice, cuts that are deeper than the accidental nick of safety scissors. My job is the care and keeping of little ones between 7:30 a.m. and 5:30 p.m.

And yes, it is really hard to accept the limitations of what an early learning professional is and does. But once you have a real understanding of it, your job suddenly becomes somewhat less stressful, and that lets you be more creative in your lesson planning or whatever it is you do.

The thing that most struck me about Malachi's mom is how inconsistent she was with his origin story. She was very consistent with wearing fantastic shoes and dressing him in wonderful clothes. I appreciated that she brought him in jammies and all his play clothing was comfortable. She didn't dress him like a little adult. I have grown to appreciate things like that.

Malachi's legs hadn't developed the same strength as other boys his age. He didn't care to crawl. He was content with sitting.

Even though Malachi was in my program for nearly three years, I never really found out how he came to be (aside from the obvious) or what his real story was—how mom met dad and what their relationship was like. They seemed to be from different paths even though they lived in the same area and unmarried. She worked as a supervisor in the hospitality industry, and Malachi's father was in and out of work. She was careful in everything she did and calculated in her personal life. His father was not that way at all.

Not meeting fathers is common for me. I would rather have one or the other parent as a client. Of course, I prefer to meet both at least once so I have a better picture of the child's life. But I no longer require an initial meeting with both parents.

But what I do wonder about is why Malachi's mom wouldn't settle on a story. One day, she would say Malachi's dad was wonderful, attentive, and doting. She showed off a bracelet he gave her and described a family dinner he planned. Another day, she would talk about cruel words—his comparing her to other women and telling her how dumpy she was. Sometimes, she said he had a beautiful home, and sometimes he lived in low-income housing.

And that is why I really wanted to share Malachi's story. Because now I do understand his mother telling two stories. I am impressed that she maintained both stories for so long and that I still don't know which was true. I have certainly seen people be kind and cruel, but the housing situation was odd to me. In any case, my job was to care for sweet Malachi and help him through his developmental issues, which were becoming more evident. His mother's first concern was his size, which was completely normal. But fairly early on, I noticed he did not move with the same ease his peers did or make the same babbling sounds. He was content to be immobile and simply watch his world pass by. Once these concerns were noticed by his pediatrician, things started changing for our daycare culture and routine. The feeling of awkwardness became persuasive and I didn't feel completely in my own element. It started in such a gradual manner that I hadn't noticed it until it became unbearable.

What does awkward mean to you? How does it feel? For me, it is unease, discomfort, foreboding. It is a feeling that boundaries have either been crossed or are about to be crossed, and I have no control of the situation. That is how I often felt when it came to Malachi. I always had a not-right feeling with his mom that was never resolved.

People say, "I bent over backwards for that person, and they did nothing for me." Well, after going to networking events with other daycare providers, I've realized I tend to go too far serving my clients, and that was true with Malachi.

Imagine walking around the daycare in a half-squat for an hour and a half following a two-year-old, trying to keep any mess out of the cell phone frame, and trying to get sweet Malachi to follow the soft-spoken prompts of a physical therapist on the other side of the Zoom call. Her top priority was to get him off his bottom, to pull up onto the couch, exercise his knees, and increase his strength to lift his not-so-light body off of the floor. He had accomplished so much working with his therapist in person before the COVID lockdowns. He was able to get up, to step away independently, and to move toward accomplishing so many milestones within the larger milestones.

Once the therapist was no longer able to come to my home, everything changed. Malachi's interest in his sessions was entirely gone. No matter how sweetly she spoke to him or enthusiastically she waved, he didn't notice her eager voice or kind smile—which made me even more desperately determined to make those sessions happen.

Such an enormously lonely feeling comes over me when I remember how it felt following Malachi around with my cell phone.

I wanted desperately to make his mother happy, to feel more secure in herself as she raised a boy who was behind his age group in development. Giving parents confidence is one of my number-one goals because it makes me miserable to see parents suffering from the lack of it.

Parents already carry the burden of the world on their shoulders, so to have a possibly disabled child only makes everything so much harder. That feeling is compounded so many times over when the parents are not together. I often forget I am a mother too, suffering under that load, and then I add to that load the weight of so many other parents that I lose sight of myself sometimes.

Not only did I want to please Malachi's mother, but I wanted to impress the young physical therapist, and all the while I was constantly thinking about what the other children might be getting into while I was following Malachi around. I also did not want the camera to pick up messes that might be here and there; I wanted to appear like I had a perfectly clean home. I also worried about the other children getting into the frame and completely ruining the Zoom therapy session, so I had to find a way to silently and kindly move them.

Following, following, following.

Ever in a half squat, ever hoping the physical therapist wouldn't notice this or that perceived imperfection in my dear daycare. What I wish I had realized then was I did not need to provide perfection. When you pressure yourself to be perfect, the world gets ever so heavy, your legs get ever so sore, and a day that could be wonderful, caring for a beautiful toddler named Malachi, can become absolutely miserable and completely lonely.

That therapy experience happened every week with Malachi. But because I wanted to be impressive and accommodating, I enthusiastically agreed to it; of course I wouldn't mind because Malachi was a priority. What I didn't realize was that meant the other children were not as important. Truthfully, Malachi was not more important than them. He got more attention because he had a developmental delay. He was special because...well, he was special because he had two stories.

By saying yes, I didn't realize I was saying it was okay for me not to watch the other children during those therapy sessions. At the time, I was also homeschooling my three children who couldn't be in school due to COVID lockdowns. My husband was upstairs working from home, and I felt pressure to keep the house especially clean so the environment would be as low-stress as possible for him. Basically, I had set myself up for failure. I think that experience is what gave me the resolve to teach people how to find peace in their jobs and lives.

If my client and her baby's therapist had known what a toll it was taking on me, they would never have asked or allowed these sessions to continue. In fact, it was the therapist who changed the plan. Before the sessions started and at the end, I would flip the phone back to me so she could tell me what she had observed and give me the homework I needed to do with Malachi to keep his progress on the track. One afternoon, the therapist asked if I was okay. Even though I tried to smile, she could tell I was barely holding on. She was the first person to have asked me how I was for a long, long while, and just that moment of concern was enough for me to break down. Thankfully, I didn't break into tears on Zoom. But after that, the physical therapy sessions took place while little Malachi was at home. Even though Malachi's attention just wouldn't focus on the therapist, she had the keen awareness to know I was overburdened and just a touch away from burnout.

That is what bending over backwards needlessly looks like. It took another team member (what the physical therapist really was) noticing what I couldn't notice and what the parent didn't have the opportunity to see. I share this story hoping you will see burnout coming if you get to where I was.

Self-care is immensely important. If we do not practice self-care, we cannot care for little ones and families as we should. When we take a moment to think about the immense difference we make as childcare providers, how responsible we are for, and the intense degree to which everyone relies on us, we see we have to take care of ourselves.

On social media, I occasionally post pictures of myself now and back in 2020 when I started investing time and money into learning about self-care. The difference in a single year is absolutely astonishing! My daycare clients will tell you I look entirely different from when they started working with me.

When you stop talking or reading memes about self-care and act by enrolling in classes that help you grow and seeking out other personal development activities, change actually happens.

When you, whether a parent, daycare teacher, or caregiver, take the same care of yourself as you do the little ones, everything will change. Today's adult world does not teach us how to find and live in a peaceful headspace. Somehow we get the message that we are not worthy unless we are overtaxing ourselves.

And so, remembering the toddler Malachi, I give you, dear reader, the profound challenge to sign up for a program that teaches you how to grow as a person in one direction or another. Sign up for that art class you never thought you could take because you believe you're not artistic. Sign up to tour the city to learn about where you live. Sign up to learn about yourself through a mentorship program.

Do something—build a story for yourself.

Journal Prompt

1.) Describe a time when you lost sight of your boundaries.

Project

Document an hour of your morning with your child or a particular child in your classroom at a half-squat like I did. Would you then think yourself into knots and question everything you ever believed in but hide it with a brilliant smile hoping no one sees through your happy facade? This is all connected to Chapter 23: Where Broken Hearts Go.

"Vulnerability is not knowing victory or defeat; it's understanding the necessity of both; it's engaging. It's being all in."
— Brené Brown

Chapter 26

A Boy She Loved Very, Very Much

"And she loved a boy very, very much—even more than she loved herself."
— Shel Silverstein, *The Giving Tree*

For every childcare provider, there is one child who changes everything. For me it was Jaxson.

Jaxson was the completion of my heart. He came to my daycare when I was in the thralls of loneliness, and I now give him credit for keeping my in-home daycare going for so long. Remembering the strength both Jaxson and I gave each other simply by so much needing company at a hard time has enabled me to see how needed caring childcare is. It was not sadness that pushed me on; it was seeing that sadness can dissipate.

Jaxson needed me as much as I needed him. He came to my daycare from the hospital at six days old, and he came without a parent. He came with the blanket and clothes Social Services gave him. He smelled musty, and he was very oily. He didn't cry; he screamed like a cat.

Jaxson's mother handled pregnancy differently than many women. She didn't carefully take her prenatal vitamins, watch what she ate, keep a calm mind, or avoid stress. She didn't take selfies or sing to her growing belly. But she did not do what some women in her situation do; Jaxson's mom chose life.

His mother took crack cocaine when she was pregnant, she drank heavily, she moved from home to home, and slept outside, alone and lost in the world. I do not know if she even knew she gave birth to him, or if her heart broke when officials took him from her with no new home ready.

No mother waited for Jaxson, no foster mom. Two foster moms had backed out when they learned about his face, his cry, and how stiff his body was.

But to me, baby Jaxson was perfect. Baby Jaxson screamed when my heart wanted to scream. And he calmed down completely when I held him tightly to me. The world and daycares would fall away from my mind as I sat with him, walked him indoors and outdoors. I completely followed my instincts and cared for him with the same concern and intention I did my biological children. And I think that may be what calmed him and enabled him to start growing calmer and thrive.

This book is about makings, about belonging, and about learning through play. And, really, this book is also about finding healing in unlikely places. That is what Jaxson did for me and, truly, what I believe I did for Jaxson.

Malachi, the boy with two stories, stayed in my program for the first three years of his life, as did many children who came to me as infants but lived farther away. Such was not true for Jaxson. Four months after starting with me, he was taken away by foster parents who did not like the bond I had developed with him, and I never saw him again.

One of the greatest aches of the childcare industry for me over the years is simply not knowing what happened. Another is being unloved by the guardians of the children I love.

Four months after Jaxson was placed in my care, he was removed by the foster parents Social Services had found for him. They were the sixth couple to consider caring for Jaxson and the one that didn't back out after meeting him. Truly, I do not understand how people could back out on what had become the most beautiful baby.

"He is our son now, and we have decided he is ready for solid foods." This was exactly what the angry foster mom yelled at me three days after he was placed with her and her husband. What if I had decided to go against my parent policy and the guidance of the USDA Food Program and simply feed sweet Jaxson puréed food because of his underdeveloped body? What if I hadn't advocated for him? Would they have kept him in my care? What if I had stopped holding him so much so he wouldn't smell like me when she picked him up? What if I had thought to call the social worker to tell her what was going on? What if? What if I had known they were not allowed to remove him from my care without the tribe's permission?

The truth was I did none of those things. Rather than all of those things, I fought her, saying I wouldn't feed him baby food at four months. I was going to follow the guidance of experts, that I was going to hold him. In the end, I felt defeated and sad and decided to treasure the days I had left with him.

Six months after they removed him, I came home to find three social workers at my door. They had so many questions. They wanted to know where Jaxson was. I did not know the foster parents did not have the authority to remove Jaxson from daycare.

I do not know what happened next, if the social workers took him from those foster parents for doing something they weren't allowed. I do not know if he was moved all over the state from home to home as other foster children I have worked with had. I simply do not know. But I do know that I loved Jaxson and took the best care of him I could.

It doesn't happen as often as you would think, but some children break your heart. For me, a few children broke my heart a little bit when they went home for the day. With Jaxson, I never wanted him to leave. I wanted to keep him near me always, but that isn't the way of childcare. Children can't find belonging with you in a lasting way, only momentarily.

Jaxson would be finishing elementary school now. There is nothing I wish more for him now than that he has found belonging somewhere like he did here. And it really does not matter if he remembers the white woman on the reservation who loved him with all her heart. What matters is his heart, his story, and the man he becomes.

In the hard and lonely, empty moments of planning and pursuing my future in serving families, I think back to helping the boy I loved very much. His cries were hard for other adults to deal with, but I knew how to wrap Jaxson up in a swaddling blanket, press him close to my chest with his precious ear close to my lips, and talk softly to him. He would slowly close his eyes, blink them open, smile, and then drift back to sleep. I would lay him down ever so gently to let him sleep and then start all over again in under two hours. Even though he was not with me for very long, his memory and picture have kept me moving forward when I was close to giving up.

The memory of holding Jaxson so close, wrapped up in his blue and white, muslin blanket, and whispering "Hush" in his ear has been such a comfort to me through my harder years. He needed me as desperately as I needed him over those six months. It wasn't baby fever; it was the need to be needed so entirely.

Some directors and classes for directors say not to hire needy people. You are supposed to hire people who are whole and complete without baggage. That is simply not what I was…or truthfully, who I am today. Are any of us?

Journal Prompt

1.) As an adult, what is hard for you to take in childcare…or really in any aspect of your life?

2.) Do you think it was smart for the foster parents to back out, knowing they couldn't deal with the cry of a "drug baby"?

3.) What would you have done were you in my shoes?

4.) Is there a child in your past whose story propels you forward?

Project

Create an action plan for dealing with a situation like I was in with my beloved Baby Jaxson. I still don't know what I should have done.

Chapter 27

Taking the Time to Fly So High with a Charity

"My whole goal is to keep my spirit intact. If that doesn't happen, none of this is worth it."
— Jewel

As busy adults we miss so many details. Perhaps being busy is the worst thing in the world. When I was in college earning the Early Childhood Education credits I needed to qualify to work as a lead teacher, I was required to work in a program with a higher degree of excellence. At the time, we only had one in the whole area, and while they did not have an opening, they accepted volunteers. It was the first and only time I really could freely play with children without having to control the classroom.

Even though you may not think it, licensed, in-home daycare teachers do not have the freedom I had in those months as a volunteer at the Birchwood Child Development Center. Twice a week, I got to work in the four-year-olds' classroom for three hours a day. I got there as they were finishing up their rest time, transitioning into snack, cleaning up, and getting on their outside things. And I would leave right after getting everyone back inside.

Charity was a little girl at Birchwood who often wanted to play with me. At first, she was very quiet and did not talk much beyond slipping her hand into mine and asking me to follow her to the swing set. After doing a little jump to get herself onto the swing, she would ask me to push her, and we would swing in silence.

Each time I came to the classroom, Charity became more and more chatty and lost all her shyness. Some days, other kids joined us, and on the days when Charity was not there, I was easily invited to play by other children.

But one Thursday afternoon in May, I was kind of sad because it was the end of my time volunteering at Birchwood. I was finishing Spring Quarter, which would complete my ECE (Early Childhood Education) classes. The winds of change were blowing, and I had the itch to move again.

Charity was there that day, but she did not ask to play with me. She did not want to eat the snack she usually rushed through. She insisted she didn't know how to put on her coat, and she didn't want to swap out her slippers for her shoes. (I loved that school's use of slippers and wish other programs would do it.) Charity wanted to fuss that day, and the lead teacher had no patience for it. She had a male teacher pick up Charity in her rest blanket and set her down on a chair outdoors behind the teacher. Then she told Charity she needed to stay there until she complied.

This behavior was so uncharacteristic of anything I had seen at Birchwood, and I was inwardly quite upset. Despite the lump in my throat, I moved past the pouting (and just-so-slightly shivering) Charity with the group of children who were holding my hands and eagerly guiding me to the swing set. I mechanically pushed five swings simultaneously while I missed my little friend and hoped she wasn't feeling lonely.

Once the children moved on to another activity, I gathered my courage (I was a very meek and shy young lady then) and asked the lead teacher if Charity could be released from her chair. By the time I got to Charity, she had her coat on, was zippered, and had her Velcro shoes on both feet. She was still looking down listlessly and appeared a bit tired. The lead teacher just nodded and let me take Charity's hand. Then we walked quietly just as we had that first day.

I did not ask my friend what was wrong, and no children joined us. I just waited for her little jump to get onto the swing and that little moment as she settled herself, and then I gave her the first little push so she could start pumping.

Instead of chattering away about what she had made at craft time or playing in free play, she started singing ever so softly a song I had taught her, "Flying oh so high, up above the mountains high, flying oh so high, up above the mountains high…."

It was the same song I used to sing when I was three with my brothers and sisters. We had made it up and sang it whenever we were driving at night. It was so haunting to hear it come from Charity on that May afternoon on my last day at Birchwood Child Development Center. And so, because I felt so much empathy for the lack of belonging she seemed to be feeling, I joined her in singing that odd, soft song.

"Flying oh so high, up above the mountain so high."

I knew that day was special. As soon as I got home, I wrote on my blog about the unlikely experience I had at one of the most highly accredited early learning programs in the area.

Just two months later, I was, myself, flying so high above the mountains, moving to Colorado Springs. I would move six more times before returning there with a confused and broken heart, looking for another making, a new belonging.

I am so glad I took the time to swing with little Charity. I am glad for the many hours of conversation with her, learning what it was like to be her. In many ways, she gave me the momentary sense of belonging I had only found in the little ones I cared for.

Journal Prompt

1.) Why do you feel Charity's story is so important?
2.) What can be done in early learning programs so the Charitys of the classrooms can be heard?
3.) Does this story inspire you to include volunteers in your program?
4.) As a child, did you have a senseless song you sang that gave you comfort?

Project

Create or find a song you can use with little ones who are having a hard time. I have done this so often over the years. It is so therapeutic and helpful to the child and me. A huge lesson I learned over the years is that music is not only for those whom others celebrate as being musical.

Chapter 28

Connor's Sister: Noticing Children Who Don't Cause Any Trouble

"Vision is the art of seeing what is invisible to others."
— Jonathan Swift

Her name was Allison, but no one really knew her by name or even noticed her. Everyone knew who Connor was, though. He was the child every teacher was scared of. He was the boy the director didn't know what to do with. Connor was the boy who belonged nowhere.

Birchwood Early Learning was a beautiful childcare facility. It was the first place where new graduates of Whatcom Community College applied. It had its own grant writer and always seemed to have the most beautiful supplies and interactive material. Birchwood Early Learning had been featured in parent magazines and was on early learning blogs. I was so pleased when I was called in for an interview, and I was even more thrilled when I was offered the position of assistant teacher in the prekindergarten (four-year-old class). This was in my early years as a daycare teacher.

But I've learned that every single school has something they don't tell anyone. Birchwood Early Learning was proud of not giving up on the kids other programs expelled. While that is a wonderful sentiment, it made Connor's sister Allison invisible.

As I've mentioned before, I always find it interesting how teachers look at parents. Connor's dad was super-cute. He was tall, but not super-tall, tan, and had blue eyes. He always dressed well. I don't know what his job was, but every morning, he was nicely put together and completely calm and polite with the teachers and director. In retrospect, that may have been the only reason Connor was allowed to continue at Birchwood.

Allison and Connor's mother looked exhausted, discouraged, and spoke like she was used to being talked over or interrupted. Just like her husband, she was very polite to the teachers and directors and patiently listened to the reports on her son's misdeeds.

I was the assistant teacher in Connor's class. After a few months of our working together, the lead teacher became pregnant and ended up taking days off. The substitute teacher worked all of the classrooms, but she could not deal with Connor's hyper-activity or the way he got distracted, disrupted others, and then went into a rage. So, she started coming up with excuses not to work in the four-year-old classroom. She was replaced by the director herself to keep the student-to-teacher ratio within regulations.

Connor was then periodically put in his sister Allison's class, and she was moved into the younger class (she was a pre-kindergarten student). The natural question here is: Why were the two siblings kept apart? The simple reason is he continually picked on his sister, disrupting all of her play and interactions with others. She was also older, so moving her disrupted her class time.

Allison's teachers pointed out that it was unfair for her to be missing out on class time and that Connor was disruptive to their older, more structured classroom. The director then tried to put him in the toddler classroom. That was a quick no from the toddler teachers who were already dealing with two biters.

I really enjoyed the times Allison was in my classroom. She eagerly offered to help with the younger kids, to clean the chairs, wipe down tables, and help with whatever we were working on.

I was less pleased when working with her brother. Most days, we had been patiently getting him through the day and inwardly celebrating that he was going to move up to the pre-kindergarten class the following week. He had absolutely refused rest time and had been just loud enough to prevent everyone around him from resting. So that Monday morning, when things are often hectic due to inconsistent home routines, I felt relief in knowing he had moved up to the five-year-old classroom.

Every teacher has a breaking point and I reached it that day when his new teacher tried to return Connor to my classroom. My day had started at 7:30 a.m. with buttering toast sent down from the kitchen and passing around a bowl of cut apples with cinnamon to the children. Connor and his new teacher arrived just as I was spritzing down the table.

"I don't want him!" I told the teacher as soon as I saw Connor. Every person has a phrase that sets them off. This was that phrase for the teacher who tried to pass Connor along to me late that Monday morning. I had already had a hard morning because I had two new students. While they had done well, new children are stressful because I had to be really clear with every step of the day so they would feel included. So, I was not up to being gracious over Connor being passed along to me.

"I don't want him," was not said maliciously or intended to be deeply hurtful the way the other teacher perceived it. I simply did not want Connor to disrupt the day.

Perhaps this chapter could be about controlling our emotions to help grow a sense of belonging with more challenging students. Maybe it could be about going with the flow in a way I was unable to do as a younger teacher.

Connor did spend the rest of his day in the class he had graduated from, and as you can guess, that meant my day did not get better. My support teacher needed a potty break as soon as Connor arrived, and just minutes after she left, all heck let loose. Connor had slipped into the art area that had "safety" scissors, opened them, and started chasing kids with them.

When I called his name and told him very directly to put down the scissors, he turned them on me and did not slow down.

My clients today tell me they cannot believe how calm I am with my in-home daycare children. My Monday experience with Connor and those safety scissors is one of the many things that gave me that patience. With a frame of reference like Connor, anything else pales in comparison.

Connor's parents and sister Allison always seemed to be trauma-free. We could see no reason for his rage or erratic behavior. Perhaps if they interacted with me as I am today, someone who looks old enough to be the one in charge, I would have learned more about Allison, the girl who was often forgotten. Her story was very intertwined with her brother's, so much so that I don't know whether it was her or Connor who was further along in their journey to belonging.

Today, they would both have graduated from college, and like with every child, I have dedicated my thoughts and energy to, I hope they have peace in their hearts. Lives are made up of moments and private thoughts. A day is made good or horrible by our first thoughts every morning.

I am curious to know how I would have dealt with all of these situations now as an older teacher with so many more experiences and a better understanding of how others think. Yes, people are complicated, but they are also all motivated by the need to belong, to be included and to be seen.

Journal Prompt

1.) What do you think would cause a child to be so disruptive that their sibling(s) would go so unnoticed?

Project

Think about an action plan for children who cause havoc—something better than passing them from teacher to teacher.

Chapter 29

Jessica, the Girl Who Didn't Have Enough

"Believe in yourself, listen to your gut, and do what you love."
— Dylan Lauren

Early learning providers are taught to look for so many things. And yet, we often become so busy complying with requirements that we don't see what is directly in front of us.

Jessica was the middle child in her family. She had an older and younger brother. Her older brother was in our school-age program and the younger brother was in the older toddler class. Jessica was in my four-year-old class at Birchwood Early Learning.

The three siblings had been enrolled at the school for a month before I started working with Jessica. I was the first teacher to notice something was different between Jessica and her brothers. The boys were confident, well dressed, had nicely styled hair, and were a little bit pudgy. Their eyes were bright, and they spoke clearly. Jessica made eye contact, but she had little energy, hardly spoke, had a very thin face, and her hair was rarely combed. Her clothing was too short around the ankles, worn, and discolored. She never had more than a light sweater.

Despite being very thin, Jessica did not finish her servings. She would wrap up food in her napkin and sneak it over to the cubbies, which were close to the dining area. She would also hang close to the teacher at outdoor time or stay inside on chilly days if given the chance.

After a week of consistently noticing this behavior from Jessica, I brought my concern to the director that perhaps Jessica was being targeted by her parents. She dismissed my thoughts, saying I was assuming the worst. Jessica's family was well dressed, well mannered, and respected the school's policies. Simply put, her family had found belonging at Birchwood Early Learning. Because they fit the profile of the school's ideal client, Jessica was unseen just like Connor's sister. But Jessica was very, very different from Allison. Allison was well cared for. She was just unnoticed by the teachers because her brother was such a challenge and so very loud.

Children's Protection Services teaches early learning professionals that if they suspect child abuse in any form, they need to report it. The teacher's job is not to be the investigator, but simply to identify and report to those who are certified and trained to investigate; a daycare teacher is required to report any sign of abuse. No "just" about it!

The director told me I was not to make the call, so I did not, even though I had taken notes on what I had observed for a week. However, when Justin picked me up from work that Thursday afternoon, I told him all about it. Because he worked for the state at the time, he was also required to report any possible child abuse.

Justin told me that by not calling Children's Protective Services a week earlier when I first suspected abuse and neglect, I had become liable if she was injured or died. That night, I called the abuse hotline, and in the morning when I arrived at work, I was immediately called into the director's office. She was very upset with me and questioned whether I should continue as a lead teacher at Birchwood Early Learning. However, after CPS talked with me, my assistant teacher, and the director, I most certainly kept my position. CPS informed us I was in the right and every teacher was required to do as I had.

After Children's Protective Services stepped into Jessica's life, things did start to change. She continued on as a student, but such a huge difference came over her aside from the obvious. She came in clean, new clothing; eventually, the gaunt look in her face faded; and she took interest in playing with the other children.

Even now, more than a decade later, I feel I could have done more for Jessica. I will always remember the horrible feeling I had when I walked out of the director's office that day knowing that I had been told not to do something I knew was right. And I am still confused about why the director did not want me to report Jessica's situation.

Jessica did not have enough, and neither did I years earlier when I had worked at Comfort Care Learning Center.

If I could go back into every one of these stories as the me I am today, I have so many things I would change. And the main thing I think I would give is food and kind words of assurance. "Keep at it. Things will get better. The teacher will notice."

Be the change for every Jessica. Today, I also wonder about her brothers. All these years later, I wonder how they are doing. Did Jessica catch up to them developmentally? Did they develop kind spirits? I think kindness is taught by showing kindness.

Despite what happened in this situation, Birchwood was a very good school, and I would highly recommend it to any family and tell any applicant that being on their staff would be an honor indeed. I've shared this story to show that not every director makes the right call, but that does not make them or the program a bad program. It is easy for even the best teacher not to see what is plainly in front of them. That is why it is important to have a coworker or a coach who comes in occasionally (as has been the case for me owning my daycare in my home with no other staff).

I am honored to have had the opportunity to work at Birchwood.

Journal Prompt

1.) Why do you think the director of Birchwood was upset that I called Children's Protective Services?
2.) Would you have done what I did?

Project

In this chapter, the way I talked about ideal clients sounded negative, but it is important to understand who your ideal client is. When you start a business, find a medium where you can reach people and tell them it is important you know who they are. Right now, describe your service and then work out who your people are. Enjoy!

Chapter 30

The Words That Saved Me

"Success is not measured by what you accomplish, but by the opposition you have encountered, and the courage with which you have maintained the struggle against overwhelming odds."
— Orison Swett Marden

"Did you know your account was in the red?"

"Ma'am, there is no good in giving up. You need to live another day. Things will get better.... Are you okay, ma'am?"

I never saw him again after that night when he told me to hang on another day. There are so many reasons for homeless individuals to move on, but I still believe all these years later that he was the angel I needed then.

I didn't really mean to kill myself that night. I have had times when I have slipped so low, or perhaps "so deep" into depression that I simply couldn't see a way out, or even, perhaps, how I got in. One thing after the other led to where I was in my mind that night. Everything felt so hopeless. I got a paycheck every other Friday, and even though I was so very careful every single day, my account was either empty or in the red when I went to deposit the next check. It wasn't about getting ahead; I was simply trying to stay afloat. And that didn't seem possible at times.

A young woman at the bank with long blonde hair and a beautiful, clean, wonderfully coordinated outfit had asked if I knew I was overdrawn. She had greeted me with a smile and remembered my name was Sarah. When I had walked to the bank that chilly evening, my head was low because I knew my check was not enough to buy good food. It would be enough to pay my rent, buy a new bus pass, and get the sanitary napkins I needed. Yes, I knew my account was in the red. It was because I needed jeans, which I got from Goodwill, and my water bill was due. At $7.50 an hour, I just wasn't making a living in upstate New York in 2004.

When I deposited my check, my account was out of the red. After paying rent, I had $17 left to buy two weeks of groceries. I lived on leftover food from the daycare (Comfort Care Learning Center), dented cans from the grocery liquidation store, Top Ramen, off-brand cereal, eggs, and imitation cheese.

The words of encouragement above were offered by a homeless man I passed by every night on my walk home from daycare. Even though I didn't plan to kill myself that night, I was drifting into a dark place in my mind I had never experienced before or since. I truly do think, though, that the memory of his words saved me—saved me in that they have been a frame of reference as I spoke of earlier. Perhaps the way we live is truly built on memories and frames of reference.

That is why writing this book is so very important.

We have all had experiences that built us into who we are. My hope is my humble book will prompt someone to dig back into their earlier years and find those frames of reference. Finding them really and truly causes us to grow!

I am immensely and forever thankful for the beautifully-put-together bank teller at the Wells Fargo branch in Guilderland, New York, and for the homeless man on the corner who played the saxophone even on cold nights. He did, indeed, save me. I only hope to be the voice in someone's life and give them even a moment of hope like I was given that night.

Journal Prompt
1.) Write about a time when you felt hopeless.
2.) Did someone without a name give you a word of encouragement you needed and then simply disappear when you looked back?

3.) Did this story empower you, or do you simply feel glad that Sarah Taron made it out of those early years alive?

4.) What small thing can you do that may be life changing for someone who is struggling?

5.) Do you have to see someone is struggling to save them?

6.) Do you believe in angels?

Project

Brainstorm about how to help someone who is in a hard situation you used to be in. For me, that might be giving a bag of necessities and a kind word to people on the street who need it.

Chapter 31

Finding the Reason for What Moves You On

"Bad things do happen; how I respond to them defines my character and the quality of my life. I can choose to sit in perpetual sadness, immobilized by the gravity of my loss, or I can choose to rise from the pain and treasure the most precious gift I have—life itself."
— Walter Anderson

Everyone experiences grief and loss.

Even as a young child, as I discussed in Chapter 1, I experienced loss when my mom went away to have my younger sister Evie Grace. My grandmother's love as she helped my dad keep everything going drove me forward. At three, I wasn't at all aware of this, but as time goes by and we age, it becomes more and more evident how needful it is to have something that propels us.

The theme of my early years was moving on and on and on and on and on. I often moved from address to address . Now, as I write this book, I am in year thirteen of running a licensed, in-home daycare. The time between graduating college and starting my own daycare was only five years. That time formed me as an adult, and it seems that so much happened during it. I can't count how many children I gave my heart to. Indeed, I can't remember many of their names or stories, but I remember the love I gave them every day and how much I hope they have found where they need to be.

Was there a reason I needed to keep leaving and starting again? I know for sure why I left Colorado Springs. I left Tristan, a wonderful man who was ready to be more than a friend. I left New York because I wanted to be home, but then I found home wasn't my place anymore.

Writing this book has been transformative for me. It has given me a safe place to truly explore my story in a way without judgment. I have been given the opportunity to have a unique viewpoint on my life. I have described this process to my husband as seeing my life from almost an outside view.

What, indeed, has pushed me from story to story? Has fear moved me on? Or, perhaps, it has been curiosity that has kept me on the move? Is it the thought that there is something better further down the road? And there keeps being the question of: Am I going to keep moving on? That question terrifies and thrills me. I would like you to allow yourself a moment right now to think about that too.

Journal Prompt

1.) Do you have an early memory of loss? What got you beyond that feeling?

2.) As an adult, do you feel you have found some "thing" or "why" that drives you forward?

Project

Create a mind map of your priorities.

Chapter 32

Tuesdays

"I don't want it good. I want it Tuesday."
— Jack L. Warner

Everyone has a favorite day, a day when they are the most productive, most receptive to directions, and know how to receive input even if it is dumb. Everyone has a day when they are impervious to distraction and discouragement. A day when upset customers just don't get to them as much.

For me, that day has almost always been Tuesday. Tuesday is not the first day coming after the weekend. Monday in the world of daycare is (almost) always a challenge because regardless of how awesome their home life, children are switching to a different routine, which can lead to grumpiness. Though it may be a bit embarrassing to admit, such is true of me too!

My wish for everyone is to find something they are completely confident in. For me, that safe place has always been daycare, especially my own daycare, Gooseberry Childcare.

Gooseberry Childcare is my creation and offering of love to the world. I have fought for it, cried for it, poured money into it, and made money from it. In my years working for other daycares, I never felt the same level of belonging I have in my own daycare. In those years, however, I did feel loved and appreciated by the children and liked by the clients.

Back then, payday was not Tuesday, so I would not have to face the perfectly-put-together bank teller. Tuesday was not the day after seeing Tristan in my Colorado days. Tuesday has been the day when my pace is set for the week and where I am really clear on my goals and start seeing progress. Tuesday is when clients really are at ease and the troubles of the weekend have subsided.

People always seem like they are forever striving for the weekend, but in my years of providing childcare, I find I wait for the work week.

If your favorite day of the week is during the work week, two things may be true of you: 1) you are in the right job, and/or 2), you need to think about what is going on with your personal life that makes work preferable. I guess, for me, it has been both.

I struggled deeply to varying degrees with my personal life for much of my time providing daycare for the kids on the Lummi Reservation. Postpartum depression was very real. My husband's dislike of having other people's children in our home eleven hours a day has been a thing. He has never liked having guests over on Sundays, and I have always enjoyed having Sunday guests. But while daycare was running and he was at work in town, I was at peace because I had my routine with the daycare kids and the house was always clean for the children and ready for a licensing visit at any time. I also knew my clients respected and appreciated me, something I was never certain of or told in my marriage.

Parenting and being married are very hard sometimes. But I know how to be an awesome daycare teacher. I take heart in knowing I bless the world by providing high-quality, early learning to the community I live in.

When I was younger, I moved around a lot, like I was searching for one thing, but that thing has always been there.

Everything changed in March of 2020. Everything. The coronavirus changed the rules, changed expectations, and put limitations where I never imagined limitations would be.

To me, Tuesdays have been what creativity and potential is. And when the lockdowns started, it felt like everything was stifled, extinguished. The daycare children didn't come for six weeks, and then the time just started stretching out.

The way I served needed to change, and so did I. Tuesday went away for a while. In those days, things...well, they just changed. My perspective on marriage and parenting changed; the feeling of freedom and cheer shifted.

I wonder if for the rest of my life I will wish I had treated my children differently, been more kind, spoken more gently to my husband. I just don't know. Perhaps I need to give myself the kindness I have coached others on: Be kind to yourself; you did the best you knew how at the time. And that truly is the case for me. I did the best I could! And such has been true of every parent and spouse over the early days of the lockdowns.

And now, as I am writing my book, I truly can say that Tuesdays have come back in their glory! Tuesday was the day for the best creativity because the daycare kids are back into the rhythm of our schedule. It is the day I am back into my routine, the house is clean, and chores are getting done. By Tuesday, everything is at peace and at pace. Perhaps that is what the world needs—space to be creative and a day to celebrate it in!

So many people ask me what the secret to my energy and enthusiasm is. I could give so many potential answers. But perhaps celebrating Tuesdays is one of them!

I am glad Tuesday is back to my family, to my marriage, to my children, and to my daycare. I am glad for creativity, for rhythm, and for joy for the future. I am glad for learning, glad for play, and glad for living a more open and less-scripted life!

Journal Prompt

1.) Is there a day of the week you think is just plain special?
2.) Take some time to think about why and how you could help others celebrate it.
3.) If you could do anything on your favorite day of the week, what would it be?
4.) Why do you think it is important to notice little details about yourself like special days of the week?

Project

For one month, celebrate a day within the work week as much as people normally celebrate Fridays. Notice how your mindset toward that day changes. It really is remarkable to me.

Chapter 33

When Thinking Just Becomes Too Much

> "We look before and after,
> And pine for what is not;
> Our sincerest laughter
> With some pain is fraught;
> Our sweetest songs are those that tell of saddest thought."
> — Percy Bysshe Shelley

Do you ever feel like you are just too tired to think? Often I want to do nothing more than close my eyes, check out, and allow the world to continue without me.

Even though I have always worked in the childcare industry, which is supposed to be bright and filled with energy, I often feel a tiredness that won't lift and move on.

I have spent so much money trying to reinvent and grow myself, build my business, and inspire women. I really feel I am leading from where I am, but perhaps it would be better if I were leading from a higher point. The more I grow, the more I see how much further there is to go.

My oldest daughter is twelve right now. When I started my daycare, she was a toddler. She was never an easy child. She has broken my heart over and over. And yet she has also held me together time and again. Claire is my darling girl, and I hope her heart will not hurt as mine has.

The lesson I want for her is to know she doesn't need to go through life scared, trying to be bigger, to find importance. I wish to give her peace and the assurance that she already has everything she needs.

I have been very angry in the past. The first time I was enraged was when my mom allowed my sister Laura to take down my Duplo tower because my play time was up. I was three, and I remember it still. It gives me pause every time I let a child break down another child's project to take their turn. It sounds cruel when I say it like that, but honestly, sometimes taking care of little ones means making decisions like that so everyone gets to play. What would have happened if Laura and I had been allowed to learn through play? Would we have fought over the Duplo or found a way to play together? My mom is one of the best people I know for setting boundaries and having high expectations and consistent values.

In some parts of this book, I have tried to frame things in a sunny, positive light. But then, as I start trying to write from that mindset, ugly, sad, mean things come to mind. This is true even of my favorite childcare programs. No matter how awesome a director is, one teacher or another is bound to be in a bad place personally. It seems some teacher always pushes other teachers around, displays unprofessional behavior toward clients, doesn't dress to code, is always late, or does things perfectly but has no sense of humor. And then I remember one purpose of this book is to "tell the truth to bullshit" (as Brené Brown says).

No daycare program is perfect; even if I wanted to frame a program only positively, doing so in this book would not be honorable. Every daycare I have worked in had at least one person who made life more difficult for everyone else. At Rainbow Daycare, we had a woman who bullied me every day, and I didn't know what to do about it. Even at my own early learning program, I have been yelled at by a client. My heart has been broken by men, and I have held the hands of people who were mistreated even if it was outside of my authority to help them.

The lesson here, dear reader, is that the world does not owe you happiness. Belonging will never be given to you; you need to create it for yourself.

In *Braving the Wilderness*, Brené Brown talks about a bad experience she had as a teenager trying out for a pep team. She had deprived herself of food and learned every dance move exactly, but she was rejected simply because she wore a colorless leotard and dark shorts while everyone else was decked out in school colors. She says this event led to her idea of creating your own kind of belonging so you can brave the wilderness—the wilderness being the world around you in which everyone has an agenda.

And that is why thinking sometimes simply becomes too much. That is why I need to love honorably.

No perfect daycare exists. No perfect director exists. No perfect Mrs. Sarah exists. No perfect mom, dad, uncle, auntie, etc. exists.

I remain in the early learning industry because it isn't a perfect place. If it were, it wouldn't be for me because I would mess it up.

Journal Prompt

1) How do you or can you help kids work through the idea of sharing when that means taking apart a creation one child is proud of?
2) What should you do when you have those moments of pause, wondering if you made the right choice?
3) Does thinking ever feel like too much for you?

4) Are you an introspective person?

5) How does the quote by Percy Bysshe Shelley at the beginning of the chapter make you feel? Of all the poetry I love (including "On Children" by Kahlil Gibran), this is one of my favorite passages!

Project

Find a poem or quote that powerfully encapsulates your beliefs, post it somewhere you will see it all the time, and notice the difference it makes to your days.

Chapter 34

First Thing in the Morning

"If you have a positive attitude and constantly strive to give your best effort, eventually you will overcome your immediate problems and find you are ready for greater challenges."
— Pat Riley

Everyone has a favorite time of the day. Mine has always been first thing in the morning.

When I worked for other early learning programs, I had all different hours. My first paid position was in 2000, working five hours twice a month for a church outreach program called Mothers of Preschoolers. After that, I had full-time employment, but that was only eight-hour days, which were within three different shifts. Over the last thirteen years, with my own daycare, I have worked eleven-and-a half-hour days. The days working at other programs seem so short now, but back then, some days felt like an eternity.

Many women struggle with self-respect, with constantly putting themselves on the discount rack in so many respects. We also have the adage, "You are enough." It is stamped on endless attire, jewelry, bumper stickers, and memes. In the early morning, I feel like more than enough, like I can take on anything because I am the first one to the daycare center.

Something I loved about being one of the teachers who arrived first thing in the morning was the time it allowed to think about the day before in peace. To this day, I think that is why I give myself extra time in the morning by going to the gym crazy early. It isn't about weight loss; it is about giving myself the chance to process the day before. And that, truly, gives me peace. Perhaps, if the world gave themselves a moment to think, things would be different.

I have first-thing-in-the-morning memories of every childcare program I have worked at. Each memory is rosy and warm because the teachers who arrive early are usually morning people, and if they are not, they usually keep to themselves with their mug of coffee.

Even my memories of filling little spritz bottles with cleaning solution and bringing them to every classroom as the early morning sun comes through the windows are sweet.

For a very brief time, I worked at Rainbow Daycare as the cook. I absolutely loved setting up the breakfast carts with their trays, toasters, clean sippy cups, or whatever the individual class needed. I really enjoyed the two teachers who also helped open the facility. My favorite (because every teacher truly does have favorites) was a very energetic teacher named Kristin.

Kristin was the type of teacher whose energy you wish you could tap into. She was every child's positive memory of a Vacation Bible School teacher! She would freely give brainstorming ideas for anything without expecting you to follow through. So many daycare teachers go around waiting to be disappointed, but that didn't seem to be the case with Kristin.

Many moving parts go into starting a day well and keeping it going in the right direction. At Rainbow Daycare, I think it all came down to the director. She brought fun to every day by always having some trick up her sleeve. The first one she ever tried to play on me I spotted before it actually happened. I had stepped out of the kitchen for only a moment to get the clothes out of the tiny laundry area when I spied her getting ready to pour a cup of salt into my water bottle. When I caught her, she acted as if she hadn't been up to anything.

Journal Prompt

1) What could you change in your daily routine to make you feel like you are more than enough?

2) What do you think causes people to feel less than enough?

Project

Write out a new daily routine that starts half an hour before you usually wake up, including something that gets your circulation moving a little. Follow this routine for a week and notice the difference in your mental health.

Chapter 35

Having the Last Word

"At the end of the day, the most overwhelming key to a child's success is the positive involvement of parents."
— Jane D. Hull

A lesson my dad has always tried to instill in me is that pride is bad and it is ever present in *our* hearts. I truly believe my dad cares for and loves me and wants me to be the best I can be—but with extreme humility. I have come up with my own definition of humility. I also have a few Scripture verses about pride I often think of. One says the wise hold their peace while fools speak continuously and mindlessly. The wise listen and measure their words carefully before answering (Proverbs 17:28).

While a lot of the language in the Bible does not connect with modern ways of speaking, it is still dear to me, even though it was often quoted with the intent of correcting my behavior. And so, over time, I have tried to develop the skill of simply listening and having the humility to let someone else end the conversation.

I have had clients teach me the power of listening by their deep concern for others. I will always remember one couple. Every morning, I ask families how they are doing, how the weekend was, or if their little one slept well the night before.

While the extra moment to connect was appreciated, often it was also brushed to the side with a bit of annoyance because clients are wanting to move on to the next step of their morning. Dropping their child off at daycare is a step toward getting through the day. Taking a moment to check in isn't always appreciated.

But there have been a couple of clients who would return the concern by looking deeply into my eyes and listening with concern and concentration for me to answer my own questions of myself in exchange for their answers. It was really an interesting, unique way of communicating I had not experienced before. It is striking to be cared for at a time when you feel you have completely lost yourself in caring for others. Showing kindness is so, so powerful.

Having the last word is often a power or ego struggle that is unwittingly engaged in, sometimes deliberately, sometimes absentmindedly. But if we allow ourselves the chance to let someone else have the last word, it is amazing what can happen next. We may find ourselves being cared for in a way that, otherwise, we never would have before.

I may write more about this in a future work, but not today. That is why I plan at some point to put out another version of this book with letters, notes, and words of wisdom from people I have asked to comment on various topics I have addressed. I want *The Making of Mia* to be an eclectic work, to be a book of many voices. I have decided, though, that this version needs to be published as it is so I can sell and introduce it to the world and get the stories of these children I have worked with out to the world. As Brené Brown says, the way is hard, but the reward is great.

Many say that raising children is best done by a community. Of course, some strongly disagree, but I think children have the greatest feeling of belonging when they are in a supportive community. And I also believe mothers usually know their children the best.

It is very important to me that you do not think children need to be in a licensed early-learning program to learn through play. No, indeed. What is needed is a safe home-like environment where children have access to open spaces and fresh air.

"Children learn to smile from their parents."
— Shinichi Suzuki

Journal Prompt

1.) What matters most to you as you serve families in the early learning world?

2.) Do you ever feel the advice and directions you learned from your family of origin and continue to repeat may be detrimental or harmful?

3.) What would have happened if I had been humble in the way my dad always taught me I should be?

Project

Create a little booklet of advice to give to daycare clients or fellow parents as a gift. It really is amazing how advice given kindly can be appreciated.

Chapter 36

What Do Memories Mean to You?

"We do not remember days; we remember moments."
— Cesare Pavese

Memories are everything to me.

My twin sister is so good about keeping old photos organized. That is something I really admire since I just can't seem to do the same. But I do dearly hold memories, and as you know, memory is not accurate; it changes based on feelings and perspective.

I have chosen to alter and reframe memories often in order to keep myself going. I would like to learn if this is unique to me. But, at this point, it doesn't matter because memories are everything. I have changed some as a coping mechanism and learned that coping is more important than accurately remembering. Being understood and explaining the way I am is too much of a burden sometimes.

I often miss my earlier self as well. I miss the days in Colorado Springs as they are now in my memory. I miss long conversations with my friend Tristan. The memory of his voice is so sweet, but even more than that is the memory of the lighter burden I had on my heart.

The reality of those years was that I was paid too little to afford a safe living place or food to sustain myself. But those memories are sweet because I was not belittled; Tristan always believed in me and told me so. He was a young businessperson, an entrepreneur, and a creator of his own dream. I remember enjoying simply listening to him talk about his dreams. At the time, he didn't have the answers to everything; he didn't even know exactly how he was going to get there, but he knew where he was going.

Sometimes, maybe often, good memories work like that. Good memories are not accurate; they are the accentuation of positive feelings and the negative simply fading away. Regardless of what people's ideas around memories are, I believe remembering the good times is necessary. Those experiences make us who we are; they create our narrative and feeling around who we are.

Novelist William Gibson says that "time moves in one direction, memory in another." I really do agree; time does move in different directions, and that has been crucial for me! While writing this book, my twin sister has warned me multiple times that nothing good comes from dwelling in the past. And she is right. Staying in the past is not a good thing. But, with all my heart, I believe it is important to remember where you came from, both with gratitude and wonder. If we block out our past, there is no way to really see our growth and understand where we are going. Memories can evaporate so quickly, and that is a big reason why I have needed to write *The Making of Mia*. In this book, I have shared more than sweet conversation. I have shared in Chapter 30 about the heartbreaking experience of walking home, knowing I didn't have enough money and the power of kind words that came from a homeless person.

I have truly gotten through the hard times by living on memories. And many of those memories were of quiet moments sitting with Tristan talking about everything and nothing—just sitting together. All of that happened over a year, but it was a time when I truly felt known, seen, and loved. Our relationship was never sexual like it would have been lived inside of a movie; it was one of deeper friendship that I wish more people got to experience.

Another question I have struggled with is: To what extent should I share my memories with the world? Does the early learning community need to know about my interpersonal relationships and the struggle to create a new chapter? Yes, they do. The reason is because everyone walks through the same struggles, the same choices, the same challenges. The daycare classroom or what we bring into parenting isn't isolated; it is the full package of everything that has created us. Sadness is as important as happiness; trials and difficulties make the happy days shine brighter. That is why I needed to share so much of my life inside the pages of this book.

Early learning is about serving families, and some of those families have been through hard things or, most often, are living within those hard times. When I first started my licensed, in-home daycare, I put so much effort into looking seemingly happy. Once I reached the point where I simply couldn't pull it off and allowed myself to be more real, my clients opened up to me about their struggles, and their level of trust in me went up enormously. That is why I have chosen to do the same with you. If you see me as real, you will see that you, too, can be impactful in whatever space you fill in the world.

> "Our sweetest songs are those that tell of saddest thought."
> — Percy Bysshe Shelley

Journal Prompt

1.) Which memories propel you forward even if they do not reflect how life is today?

2.) Are the sad, challenging days as important as the easy, bright days?

3.) What do you think makes us who we are?

Mia was a small ugly brat who looked half as ugly as me and my family.

Project

Create a memory book of little things around the house/classroom. Use pictures and clippings from magazines that represent or capture a fun experience you had.

Chapter 37

What Does Moving Forward Mean to You?

"Time is too slow for those who wait, too swift for those who fear, too long for those who grieve, too short for those who rejoice, but for those who love, time is eternity."
— Henry Van Dyke

Moving forward means everything to me. In fact, it is so meaningful that I named my podcast after it! Moving forward enables us to grow stronger emotionally and intellectually, and if we are very intentional about it, it makes us kinder and more understanding.

When I tell people what my book is about, they say, "You really need to finish the book and put it out into the world." As I have written, I have come to understand that I need this book more than anyone else because moving forward terrifies me.

While I would not call myself a quitter, I have chosen to discontinue many things. As I have gotten older and accomplished more, further developing how I move on is not the same. I don't move from city to city or places of employment. But I do feel a tugging toward changing course, and that is really a scary thing for me because it means stepping into vulnerability. It is important to move on instead of pushing yourself and investing time where you are no longer interested or making real progress.

Now is the time to truly build your dream. And when it comes to writing this book, I am moving forward and investing my time because I realize what will happen if I don't share my story and the stories of the families I have served as an early learning provider. There are a lot of things I have been grinding forward in and not making real progress in (the nanny service specifically) and then other things (the in-home daycare) whose time I know have been fully served.

Good things disappear so quickly if we don't write them down. All these children matter, and so do their stories, even though I can only tell the story of one moment or a couple of years. Their joys matter, and perhaps even more, their struggles matter.

I tell these stories to help you see the importance of building your daycares, family, and wherever you interact with children into places that foster a sense of belonging.

Belonging can be so elusive, but I believe we can help children feel secure by making even the smallest changes.

If someone took the time to sit with Connor's sister (Chapter 28) and read a book to her every morning when she got to the child development center, she would probably have had a more positive feeling about her life.

And so often I think of Morgan (from an earlier chapter) whose dad had PTSD. She was so, so hard to be around because of her angry, explosive behavior. But what if, back then, I had known about better self-care practices? Would I have been able to provide a calmer atmosphere where she could have taken a nap in the morning to recover from a sleepless, chaotic night at home? What if she could calm herself enough to freely play like the other children?

Truly, I did the best I knew how to. And that is what I would like for you to know as well. I would like for you to learn from me and, indeed, from yourself. Don't doubt yourself if you haven't served children in the past well—just allow yourself to grow from that.

Journal Prompt

1.) What would you have to do to provide an atmosphere of belonging in your family or classroom?
2.) How are you practicing self-care today, and do you feel it makes a difference in how you perform your job?
3.) Why do you feel it is important to avoid beating yourself up over past missteps?

Project

Take some time to think about what your life would be like if you hadn't chosen to move on from something negative. What if you hadn't moved on from your favorite pet passing away? That really could have changed your whole life. Then reach out to me to schedule a time to come on my podcast and tell your story of moving on. But remember, to be on my show, *Stories, Inspirations, and Moving Forward*, you need to be able to teach my listeners something. That will be no problem, though, because remember: You are a rockstar!

Chapter 38

On the Other Side of the Rainbow

"I am completely happy with my life. I love everything about it."
— Julia Roberts

Have you ever felt completely at home when you walked into a business without having a particular reason why? Have you ever felt like you were in the right place at the right time? Have you ever been completely certain of something even though you didn't have a logical reason?

Yes, yes, and yes for me.

I had a good year in 2008. It was the year I applied to work at a mid-sized daycare in Bellingham, Washington, called The Rainbow Daycare. It was a daycare that believed there was promise in every single person, every child, every parent, every teacher.

When I went back to Washington, I was not in a peaceful state of mind. I had come home before I wanted to. I was in my head, questioning everything and so unsure of myself or where I wanted to be. The first step was to find a job I had become quite good at and that gave me the focus I needed. It did not take me long to notice an interesting ad for employment. Rainbow Daycare needed a teacher in its three-year-old classroom! Years before, when I was attending Whatcom Community College, I had known a few people who had worked at Rainbow and liked it, but I had never applied simply because I had not planned to stay in Washington.

I had been inspired by the story of the director who had started the childcare program even before she turned eighteen and would be allowed to own a business. Her tenacity was much the same as that of Autumn and Summer's mom whom we talked about many chapters back. I absolutely love stories where someone pushes past boundaries people say cannot be overcome.

Looking back, I wonder what would have happened if I had applied at Rainbow Daycare in 2004 when I was nineteen and had just graduated from community college. Well, I know what would have happened: I would have worked at one childcare program and had only a story of peace.

As with every good story, mine needed hills and valleys. I am glad I went to New York to work for Miss Rose and half froze to death living in unreliable housing. And I am glad I went to Colorado and worked for Miss Doris and then got to be a lead teacher at God's Light Childcare.

I read a poem a long time ago—I can't quite remember the name—that talks about a beautiful woman who starts life with a heart full of joy, taking long, confident strides, wearing beautiful clothing and a brilliant smile. As the poem continues, she sees hungry people and gives them her food. When she sees children with inadequate clothing, she makes tunics from her flowing garments. And when she meets people in mourning, she sits a while and weeps. By the end of the poem, she looks very different, but she is more beautiful for the care she has given.

Rainbow was run by a wonderful woman who truly understood how people think and what inspires them to do well. She understood that when teachers are taken care of, they will take care of children and families to an even higher degree. Not only did the director have a smile every day, but she had something clever to say and was continually playing odd tricks on us teachers. She kept what is easily a place of high stress, fun and energetic. She found fun in small things that spread and made her program truly special.

My husband thinks perhaps I had a hard time working at other daycares because I took myself and my work too seriously. Rainbow's director didn't let anyone think they were too important to be played with. I think that is the main thing I miss about being a part of her program. Life becomes so much easier if you give yourself and the world around you a break from the serious side of whoever you may be.

Just as children learn best through play, so adults also need play in their lives in order to truly do well, to love their jobs, and to enjoy the everyday routines that make us who we are.

Journal Prompt

1. Write about a time when you took yourself too seriously and how it affected your life.
2. Do you think the practice of caring for employees first could change any kind of work culture?

Project

The director spoken of in this chapter is the same woman as in Chapter 35 who tried to put a cup of salt in my water bottle. Come up with some practical jokes that you could play in your workplace…or maybe you should do them at home. Pinterest has all kinds of ideas.

Chapter 39

To This Day

"With the new day comes new strength and new thoughts."
— Eleanor Roosevelt

What comes to mind when you hear people say, "To this day?" To me it sounds like they have been through something traumatic that has brought them to a lasting resolve. I guess that is true for me at times. But in this chapter, I will talk about the first time Justin brought me flowers at work.

Oh. My. Gosh! Even now, as I write this, I am smiling.

I first met Justin at Woods Coffee, a local coffee shop, on a blind date. It only happened because I was lonely and bored one day when all of my roommates had their boyfriends over.

That is actually different from the story I tell everyone. All these years, I have told people I only went to craigslist because a roommate dared me, but such is not the case. I told the story that way because it makes me sound like less of a loner. I wasn't an outcast; I simply lived life alone. I kind of just went through life missing Tristan and living on a memory. And that, dear reader, is not what I have wanted to tell people. But now that I am writing a truthful memoir, I will tell you I answered the notice "Christian Guy Looking for Christian Girl" out of pure loneliness, and perhaps, a desperate need to take a step toward creating a new making.

On that day, I was serving lunch at Rainbow Daycare. I had been working there for several months, and the routine had become smooth and enjoyable. At the time, I had just moved from being the cook to being a full-time preschool teacher, and I was really proud of myself.

It is funny how sometimes the most exciting, thrilling things happen when you are completely focused on something else. In fact, if I look back at some calendar, it would turn out that the day my boyfriend brought me flowers for the first time was a Tuesday. Whether it was my favorite day of the week or not, it was so special!

Tristan was really the only guy I had had in my life as an adult, and he wasn't more than a friend, just as good and dear a friend as could be. I am sure that if he had brought me flowers at work, that alone would have made him into my crush. But at the time I was so busy surviving that I simply didn't see him in that way. It is funny the little things that make all of the difference. Tristan gave me the time, attention, and conversation I so dearly needed in those days. And I will forever remember him for that and be glad he was in my life. I truly believe everyone comes into and leaves our lives at exactly the times they need to. And, looking back, we need to be kind to ourselves, saying that we did the very best we knew how to do at that time.

My greatest wish for all people is not that they accomplish a certain income or housing status, but that they reach a place of peace in their hearts. Peace does not mean settling; in fact, for me peace has meant continuing forward, growing. But, growth is no longer with a spirit of desperation; it is with eager curiosity and openness. Even now as I write, this my life is in a time of transition that is both exciting and terrifying.

On that April afternoon in 2008, as I was busily setting the preschool lunch table for the children due to walk in from the play yard, the front door to the daycare center opened, the little bell rang, and a not-quite-familiar voice asked if Sarah Taron were available.

Oh. My. Gosh.

Justin says he hates his voice. He always has. But for me, at that time, his voice was the most charming sound in the world. Over time, his voice has not brought me that level of elation, but it sure did that day! And I hope each of you experience the wonderful joy I did on that beautiful April day when love was new for us. It is a moment that can become a memory that holds you through many difficult times.

The teacher standing guard at the entry said yes in a confused, surprised way and pointed at me. All eyes went to the blonde fella with a button-up shirt and slacks. There he was. He was handsome in a way no other guy ever had been. He was there for me, and the flowers he was nervously holding were for me. He was handsome then because he saw me for more than anyone else had or did. It was a kind of handsome that was not at all physical.

I don't remember what I said when he handed them to me—probably a lame "Thanks," but gosh, I took such good care of that five-dollar bouquet of daisies. The cook put them in a mason jar for me, and after lunch, I put them in my classroom by the sink. That bouquet of flowers brought me so much joy.

To this day, when Justin gives me flowers, I remember the twenty-eight-year-old version of him—so young, so vulnerable, so hopeful, and so brave. I have clung on to that memory in the harder years.

Over the years, I have been desperately lonely, overjoyed, miserably disappointed, elated out of my mind, regretful, mystified, embarrassed, stuck, and incredibly liberated. I have had many opportunities to part ways with Justin. At times, it would have just made sense and been easy. But to this day, as I write this book, we are still Justin and Sarah, together, with each other's best interests at heart.

It really comes down to where you want to be when you are hurting. Where do you truly belong when the world just isn't right? The theme of finding home where you are has continued throughout this book, and I will bring it back here. I have learned not to find home only where Justin is; it is where I am. Home and belonging can only truly be found within yourself. I hope you find this to be true in your life as well. Time and circumstances are guaranteed to change our relationships, but belonging should not depend on them. It has not been easy to reach this level of understanding. In fact, writing this book has caused me to delve even further into it. And I am excited for subsequent books to see how things have continued to evolve in my life.

We've had a lot of hard times. On our first Christmas, my gift to him cost twenty-five dollars. It was a blue sweater. This Christmas, I easily spent money on him, knowing it comes from generosity, not trying to buy his love, but rather showing him I know him.

We were living on my husband's entry-level salary and the money I made at Rainbow while scraping money together to start my own daycare. Providing childcare to our community was so important to me that I dedicated every spare moment to researching how to open my own daycare.

Two months after we got married, I was pregnant. I worked at Rainbow Daycare through my pregnancy with the understanding that I was leaving when Claire was born. I spent time doing my job the best I could. Miss Sherri, the director, took time to answer every question I had about starting a daycare.

When Claire was thirteen months old, I became fully licensed to provide daycare in our home, and by the time she was eighteen months old, we were full. And after a year of that, I got pregnant again. Two years later, I had my third and last child with Justin.

Having your own children truly does change everything. To this day, I am so thankful I decided to choose another chapter in my life. To this day, I am thankful that I decided to come back to Washington State. And I know there will be many more chapters in my life, many more times of explosive growth. And now, after writing this book, that no longer scares me. I have found belonging within myself, and now the idea of growth is exciting and thrilling. That is my wish for you!

Brené Brown says that belonging is something you need to find within yourself. If you want to explore this idea more, I highly recommend her book *Braving the Wilderness*. She has written many books, done Ted Talks, and spoken everywhere, but the first book I read of hers remains my favorite. Here is a quote of hers I really connected with throughout writing this book:

Layout indent next paragraph

> Stop walking through the world looking for confirmation that you don't belong. You will always find it because you've made that your mission. Stop scouring people's faces for evidence that you're not enough. You will always find it because you've made that your goal. True belonging and self-worth are not goods; we don't negotiate their value with the world. The truth about who we are lives in our hearts. Our call to courage is to protect our

wild heart against constant evaluation, especially our own. No one belongs here more than you.

The thought of how many different people will pick up this book is so wonderful! When I started writing, I thought it would just be for parents and daycare teachers, but as I have gone through the process of writing and talking about this book, I have gathered such a wide audience. And I know, over time, that so many more different types of people will find *The Making of Mia*.

Journal Prompt

Write about a time when you were treated well by someone and what brings the thrill of that moment back to you.

Project

Create a "blind date" for you and your spouse or significant other.

Chapter 40

When You Find Yourself in the Kitchen

"You either walk inside your story and own it or you stand outside your story and hustle for your worthiness."
— Brené Brown

At some point in every person's life, they must decide whether they are going to step out of what they are good at for something easier, or step farther into what they are doing where the work may be harder. That has happened to me many times, but most significantly in 2007.

By 2007, I had been working in childcare for eleven years. Looking back at pictures from the time, I look like a baby, but by then, I considered myself a veteran. Between my confusion about Tristan and being fired from Weber Street Daycare, I felt like maybe I wasn't meant for childcare.

When I moved to Washington, I didn't apply to be a daycare teacher; rather, I applied for a job cooking at a daycare. I just couldn't get myself all the way out of daycare. Daycare was my comfort zone, and I had good memories of Comfort Care Learning Center, God's Light Childcare, and College Way Child Development Center.

Where do you go when you need employment in a new place? That's right—you go to craigslist. Craigslist said the little daycare near the airport called Rainbow Daycare was hiring a cook. What qualified me to be a cook? Well...everything.

My twin sister and I were the second and third in a large family. Baking the bread had always been my chore. I had a lot of experience serving kids food. I had always been nice to daycare cooks in the past. I figured maybe that qualified me. Why not try? So that is what I did.

And...believe it or not, the director called me back right away and said she would like to interview me. I was more nervous than I expected. I sat up very straight, dressed in the clothes I thought an applicant for daycare cook would wear.

A lot of people talk about "imposter syndrome" in the same way and as often as they talk about "narcissism." Many are hyper-focused on these terms and the ideas behind them. If I had known those words that day, I might have claimed to feel imposter syndrome. More than anything, though, I felt a need to belong again. And I believed Rainbow Daycare offered that opportunity, so when Miss Sherri, the director, called later that week and asked when I could start—then without hardly pausing said my start day was the following Monday—I was in.

My favorite part of being the cook was that I felt like I was at the epicenter of everything. I love the first-thing-in-the-morning feeling of being at the daycare center before everyone else. I loved setting everything up for the day. I loved laying out everyone's things for the afternoon snack that would be served while I was on my way home on the bus. I loved figuring out the meal binder, sorting through the cupboards, and delving into the pantry to figure out what I could make with what was left over before the Costco order was delivered. I loved setting aside milk cartons for classrooms when they were putting together a class project. And I loved having the teachers come drink their coffee in my little area on their breaks.

One morning, Miss Sherri asked why I had left the classroom. I told her it was because I had decided it was time to move on. She asked how I would feel about going back to the classroom. She told me not to say no too quickly because she needed a teacher in the threes' class and was confident it would be a good classroom for me.

That was so long ago, and I am still not sure if she was waiting to fire the threes' teacher until she could find someone else or if I was doing a bad job as cook and she didn't want to fire me.

Two weeks later, I was in the threes' classroom decorating for Valentine's Day, and we had a new cook in the kitchen named Miss Wendy.

The best thing to do when you find yourself in the kitchen is to learn to be the best cook you can possibly be. And that is absolutely what I did. Miss Wendy was the former owner of a local bakery and she was happy cooking for a mid-sized daycare when she retired. All these years later, even though Rainbow closed, Wendy is still the cook for the daycare that took its place.

For a short time, I was in a place that wasn't ideal for me, but it was where I got an appreciation for and interest in serving high-quality meals for children.

Because of that experience, I have learned more about the child nutrition program in my area and always been an energetic host to the local representative, Miss Jeanne. She has always been so kind to me and shown true concern for each child being served in my program. One of the best tools she gave me as a new daycare provider was a wonderful meal planning template. She even sent me a copy to include with this book.

As you know so very well, every child is different from the next. I have had a few kids come through my doors who had difficulties I was just not figuring out on my own. Jeanne patiently listened and often came up with a very clever solution. We have helped kids who were so heavy they ran out of breath walking across the play yard by introducing them to unprocessed foods. We helped a girl who was gaunt by giving her more protein in her daily diet. We helped kids who were hyperactive enjoy quiet story time simply by changing their diet.

I had always known that being a cook was far more than turning out carts of food at the proper times (which is hard), but once I really took time with Jeanne to figure out how to create an awesome food program for the kids at Gooseberry Childcare, I fell in love with and gained more respect for that aspect of the childcare industry.

Working inside a daycare is my story (going back to Brené Brown's quote). I don't need to hustle to be inside of the industry. But now, after all these years, I am seeing how desperately large the industry is, how many facets there are, and how much work is yet to be done. In fact, now is probably a more-than-ever-before moment.

As I write this, the world is staring into the face of year three of the global coronavirus pandemic. Everyone is facing shortages. As all of this is going on, I am sitting comfortably at home in my empty daycare. All the children registered to attend have been out all month. I miss them, but writing this book has been so important to me because I know the world needs to hear the stories of these children, how they lived, how they loved, belonged, felt lost, felt known, felt safe, moved, and grew. I want this book to reach everyone. I want people to feel hope and know that the small things are important, that unscripted lives are good lives. Things don't have to be pretty to be good. The best things in life sometimes aren't planned, rehearsed, or purchased.

It is funny how many things I wonder about when looking back at my time working at other people's daycare centers. I have been my own boss for so many years that I find it hard to believe I could have ever dealt with other people's motivations, ways of thinking, plans, schemes, or anything.

Miss Sherri was and is a very smart, clever, far-sighted woman. She doesn't live life moment-by-moment. She sees things far in advance and enjoys the moments because she planned ahead. That is very clever and something I have tried to follow.

I'm left wondering why Miss Sherri put me in the threes' class. Whatever the story was, I am very glad for it. I was in the kitchen long enough to realize it is something I want to do again, someday, in some capacity. But it wasn't right at that time because it was just too intense. Just like so many other things in this book, there is a bit of me that wishes I could go back to that moment and try to do it better, but that is not the point.

When I was given the three-year-olds' classroom, I felt myself come back to life! Miss Sherri was wonderful, and my favorite thing about her was her openness to teaching. Whenever I had a bit of a challenge, I would ask her to observe my classroom to get at the root of whatever was going on. Other teachers avoided inviting the boss into their classrooms. And other directors might not make the time to observe unless there was a real problem, which there definitely was not. I think I wanted to decode what happened with Connor so long ago when he had chased me around that classroom at College Way Child Development Center.

After observing, Miss Sherri would give me her ideas, and I could write up a plan to increase classroom morale. And that was where I stayed until I had my daughter Claire Renee.

I am very grateful to Miss Sherri, Miss Rose, and Miss Karma for their kindness, professionalism, and for giving Sarah Taron the time of day and encouragement. It would be my very great honor to give each of them a signed copy of this book and to take them out to lunch as a thank you for seeing me when no one else did.

Journal Prompt

1.) Would you feel touched if you were asked to go back to a job you meant to move on from? For me, I am beyond grateful to Miss Sherri for seeing that my light shined the most when I was with students.
2.) How would you feel if someone came back to you twenty years later and thanked you for showing them kindness?

Project

Write a letter to someone who helped you in some way and send it to them in your own handwriting. It will mean the world—I promise!

Chapter 41

Stepping Off the Bus, Where Would You Go?

"Don't try so hard to fit in, and certainly don't try so hard to be different, just try hard to be you."
— Zendaya

Over and over in this book, I have asked, "Where do you find belonging?" I have told you how my own path was guided by this search, and I have challenged you to consider where you find belonging in yourself.

When I saw Zendaya in *The Greatest Showman*, I was fascinated first by her character in the film and then by her, her path, and how she dealt with social media in an age when a person can live or die by what the faceless say.

Zendaya's parents wanted her to commit to basketball, and she excelled at it, but her heart was called to the arts. She talks a lot about following your heart, finding home where you are, and being impervious to the ever-present pressures found everywhere, especially those faced by young people. Zendaya dresses how she wants and wears her beautiful hair how she wants. She plays insecure characters, stepping out into their worlds in brave ways others would not. In magazines, movies, and online, she puts herself in front of young girls of color who desperately need role models. Zendaya walks boldly in a terrifying world. It is a world with a global pandemic, racism, and misinformation—a world of fear.

Busses have been a big part of my life. I was diagnosed with epilepsy at the age when kids are usually going to drivers' education. Normally, fifteen is a really exciting time for kids, but it wasn't for me. It was a time of disappointment, but as you know, I do not dwell in disappointment; I keep moving forward.

Instead of drivers' education, when I was fifteen, I started classes at our local community college. I took the bus to school for the three years it took me to finish. And when I moved to New York, I got from place to place on the bus. Later, after realizing I just couldn't keep up on $7.50 an hour, I got around on a bus in Bellingham while attending college and working two jobs.

I didn't quit riding the bus until I finally learned to drive in 2008!

Bus people were my consistent friends over the years. There was no Tristan on the bus. I'm sure there was plenty of danger, but I really was safer there, more confident. You just had to be alert not to miss your stop. And often, when you did get off, it was either not quite where you wanted to be and you had to walk forward or backtrack a bit. That really is how my life had worked until that point—forward, back, past, not quite.

I didn't give up the bus altogether when I learned how to drive; my bus culture just changed, bringing a bit of trepidation with it. The bus was no longer the city bus; it became the school bus. When the school bus came, my children went away; when the school bus returned, my children did as well, but I felt I then needed to heal them from the day away from me. They needed to be fed, comforted, and settled back into my care.

When I first started the daycare, I accepted school-age kids. Their bus would arrive at three o'clock.

Masina stepped off the bus with confidence, with a smirk of a smile and a subtle skip in her step. Sometimes, she had a sad look, a slight, defiant smile. But she also always had a sense of pride and dignity.

Masina was perfectly and completely herself. She had been through hard times even before she was born. She had been moved from home to home all her life.

And, as a seventh grader stepping off the bus one November afternoon, she was barely holding on. She walked across the street in the same way she did every afternoon, with long, confident strides. But after coming through the door, she didn't speak immediately. It was as if she didn't trust her voice or was simply too angry to speak.

Instead of saying "Hey" as she did every day, she simply handed me a note in black marker with square, uniform print saying, "Masina is not to use her phone and has to read the whole time she is at daycare."

I don't know why that made me so upset, but it did. Not only did I call her foster parents, but I also went into my parent policy and added a special amendment saying that I would never adhere to such notes. My daycare was a place of respite for children of all ages, not just for infants to pre-kindergarteners.

Masina did not use her phone that afternoon. She left it in her hoodie pocket and talked with me until her foster parents picked her up. She didn't want to be on her phone, and I didn't want her to be. But I didn't want her to stay off because she had been told to by whomever wrote that note; I simply wanted to hang out with her.

All Masina's teachers were terrified of her. She took great pride in intimidating them, in yelling and being hurtful to every authority figure. Her guardian *ad litem*, counselor, foster parents, and even my husband told me she was kind and relaxed with me because I had never asserted myself with her. The heavy implication was that I wasn't doing my job properly until I asserted myself.

Truthfully, I had no desire to assert myself if it meant that Masina would yell at me. I didn't want to be terrified of her. I didn't want my feelings to be hurt. I didn't want her to be a repeat of Masina or awful like Connor. I wanted to talk with her every day. I wanted her company and I wanted to be a respite for her. Masina's life was a storm, and I wanted her ninety minutes at Gooseberry Childcare to be a period of calm.

She really reminded me of myself in so many ways.

Masina finished at Gooseberry Childcare when she turned thirteen. I reached out to the Department of Youth and Family Services to ask them to make an exception to my daycare license so Masina could continue to attend. The answer was short, and I am sure you can guess what it was.

Shortly after finishing at Gooseberry, Masina ran away from her foster parents' home. She was living on the streets until the police found her and put her in the county jail as a juvenile runaway. She was also removed from the care of her foster parents and moved to a group home.

"Shy" was the best word to describe me as a child, and even as an adult, shyness has been a character trait of mine. For Masina, I did something so far outside of my comfort zone—gathering all of my courage, I called the group home where she was placed and asked how and if I could visit.

My plan was to renew our relationship and visit her often, trying to be a respite and source of company again. I thought about it all day and had talked myself in and out of it so many times by the time the daycare closed for the evening. Then I fed my family an early dinner and headed out.

Once I got to the group home, I went to the office, told them my name, and said who I was there to visit. They called wherever Masina was as I waited. I waited and waited. After what seemed like forever, the woman who had called told me that Masina didn't want to see me—nothing she said had changed Masina's mind.

I couldn't breathe when she told me Masina didn't want to see me. All I could do was nod, sign out, walk away quickly, unlock my car door, and start crying. I felt betrayed and more alone than I had ever felt before. I felt as though all my years of working with families had been stupid. I felt like all the years I was planning for in the future were stupid. I felt limp and didn't want to do anything. And so, I sat in my car for a long time. By the time I left, the sun had set, my tears were gone, and I felt empty.

I went back to the group home three more times that month. I couldn't bring myself to walk through the doors. I just sat in the parking lot and then left without crying, without anything. Perhaps I was building resolve. Perhaps I was stepping into another mindset.

That was 2018. A month later, I closed my before-and-after-school program. As I write this book, that program is still closed and I have no plans to ever open my heart to daycare kids above the age of five again.

Masina broke my heart that year, but I let it mend. I knew Masina was still a proud girl who carried herself with dignity and would always do so. My only wish for her was that she be well. It was never truly about me.

> "Your children are not your children. They are the sons and daughters of Life's longing for itself. They come through you but not from you, and though they are with you, yet they belong not to you."
> — Kahlil Gibran

Masina belonged to tomorrow. She was not mine, though she went to my daycare. Her thoughts were and are the thoughts of tomorrow. Her values are those of tomorrow. She was and is beautifully and entirely her own, with dignity and strength beyond what anyone expected. Masina is without limit.

That year, Masina ran away numerous times. The group home I tried to visit her at would not accept her back after she ran away multiple times and incited fights. She was passed to other facilities, and the system begged her foster parents, my former clients, to take her back. They said yes for Christmases and a couple of times for longer stays, but she always ran away.

Through all this, my heart rooted for her, believed in her, and knew that one day she would find belonging within herself like I have talked about so many times already in this book.

This week, I had the great honor of talking to Masina on the phone. It has been a lifetime since I cried desperately in my minivan in front of the group home. Looking back, I think I was crying for myself as much as I was crying for her. It was the first time I had really cried over all the running away I had done in my young adult life. It was the first time I had allowed myself to grieve over a lifetime of things.

Today, Masina is the mother of a beautiful, seven-month-old daughter. She is the same age as Marissa from God's Light Daycare at the beginning of this book. It was such an honor to talk with her. I am looking forward to some day meeting her daughter. She is determined to be the mother she never had and show the strength and guidance she never had.

One idea I had for this book was to include words of wisdom from mothers to the mothers who will read this book. I came up with the idea while people were busy getting ready for the holidays so I didn't get many volunteers. But Masina said yes, and that, sweet reader, is another reason she is so cool and will go far in life. Choosing to step into something bigger when others do not is a big deal.

And so, in the bonus section, you will find a picture of the beautiful Masina and her stunning infant daughter. My wish for Masina and her daughter is the same wish I have for all the children I have been honored to care for—that she find love, belonging, and a sense of home within herself wherever she goes.

In fact, the idea of home is what made me choose Zendaya as a celebrity I wanted to endorse in my book. In an interview with *Vogue*, she said that home is wherever she is. She said it so easily, without even seeming to give it much thought. And then as I went back and listened to her work and more interviews, I realized that she truly believes in belonging in the same way I do. And so, I knew I needed to include her in this chapter as well. Masina was a girl defying all odds, finding her place, just as Zendaya talks about taking her own course fearlessly, with pride and confidence even in the hardest of times.

When you get off the bus, you never know what to expect, what you will be stepping into, how you will feel, what the weather will be doing, or what will happen in the next ten minutes.

Living with public transportation as your only means of getting around is a very vulnerable place to be. It is no wonder that I fell for Tristan.

Journal Prompt

1. Journal about a time you found yourself in a place like I did when I was fifteen, realizing you would not be able to take part in an exciting milestone in your life and needing to find another path.
2. Talk about a time when your feelings were so deeply hurt everything else felt meaningless.

Project

Look up the route you take to work or a common destination and then click on the bus route version on Google maps. If you are feeling adventurous and don't mind wearing a mask (if you are reading this during the pandemic), go experience what it is like to depend on public transportation. Yes. It sure is a different way of being.

Chapter 42

The Biggest Compliment

"The happiness of life is made up of minute fractions—the little, soon forgotten charities of a kiss or a smile, a kind look, or heartfelt compliment."
— Samuel Taylor Coleridge

I have been asked several times if anyone ever told me I look like Julia Roberts. Each time I have been flattered all over again. To me she is stunning, kind, and completely relatable; glamorous, yet so human. The last time I mentioned it to someone, she said, "Well, Julia Roberts should consider herself lucky to look like you." And then I realized beauty truly is measured by kindness and generous contributions to the world.

Have you taken time to care for someone without expecting recompense or personal gain? Have you loved without expecting love in return? That is the real measure of goodness and the greatest compliment.

The lesson my dad has always wanted to impart to me is to be humble. And yet, the compliment of being compared to Julia Roberts carried me through some hard times. It was almost as if looking like someone important meant I was going to be okay.

> "The older you get, the more fragile you understand life to be. I think that's good motivation for getting out of bed joyfully each day."
> — Julia Roberts

I am so glad you spent this time with me, hearing about Mia and so many other children I have worked with. Their stories have carried me forward as did the Julia Roberts compliment. I hope I have inspired you in some small way to look deeper into people's eyes, to listen a little bit longer, and to care for a few seconds longer than is convenient. When you give yourself a chance to care, everything changes. It really is all we need to bring about world peace.

One of my favorite writing teachers told me you have succeeded as a writer if you can take your reader completely into one scene and have them feel what it would be like to be that person entirely, to feel how they feel, to see through the eyes of that person. I hope so much that I have been able to do that for you.

I am a storyteller. I am a daycare lady. I am an advocate. I am a mommy, and I got to marry Justin. I have lived thirty-six years on this earth, and there is so much more I still want to do. I want to write more; I want to tell more. I want to meet more people. I would be honored to someday meet Zendaya, Julia Roberts, Miss

Rose from Comfort Care, Brené Brown, and the many people I have quoted throughout this book. I want to travel to and tour Ireland.

A dear friend died last week of coronavirus. The economy and so many things have been affected and forever changed due to this global pandemic. And that really is also part of the reason I needed to write this book. I needed to preserve my words and the work I have done. Other authors and early learning professionals talk about the importance of learning through play. But no one has written about Morgan and Allison, Masina and Jaxson, Jessica and Mia, sharing their stories.

Thank you for reading my book.

Journal Prompt

1.) What would a meaningful compliment be to you?

2.) Do you give compliments easily?

3.) Is it hard for you to accept compliments?

Project

Make a point to accept every compliment you receive for a week. Believe it or not, shrugging off and dismissing compliments is rude. And it makes the giver of the compliment feel kind of dumb.

Chapter 43

Active Listening Is One of the Hardest Lessons

"There is a difference between listening and waiting for your turn to speak."
— Simon Sinek

At times, I have been too shy to say anything; sometimes even the thought of entering into a conversation made breathing a little bit harder. My oldest brother would encourage me, saying, "I can tell you have something to say. Just say it."

Over the years, I have remembered his encouragement, and little by little, I have gotten braver. Now I make my money by talking, by reaching out and building other people up. I have realized that more people feel how I did than I imagined. I used to think the world had everything figured out, and I was the only one who was struggling to speak.

Have you ever felt like you just could not help but end every conversation with your own quip? After all, you are the most clever, knowledgeable person in the room. Aren't you the one they came over to talk to or invited to the meeting? Aren't you the one who wrote the book?

One of the biggest lessons I have learned is that the world is perhaps more interesting when I let my guest have the last word, let the host of a meeting be the last one to speak, or let someone else end a casual conversation. Sometimes I intentionally take the part of a listener in my podcast, and those are often the best shows.

With all my heart, just as I believe every person is an artist or mathematician, I believe everyone is a writer. The journal will help you capture the stories and essence of each child within your care.

Each child has their own story even if they have the same parent. I could make this book at least three times longer were I to include the parents and siblings' stories as I did for Miss Julia (Mia's mommy) or the daddy who's heart had been broken, or the sister who was unseen, or the parents of the girl with two stories, and so on.

In many of these stories, I was in the wrong. Throughout my life, I have had times when I was not the hero. I have not always stepped up when I should have. More than once, I have acted without integrity. I have hidden when I should have fought or fought when I should have stepped back.

The reason I include all of this is because I want you to see my making, my education, and my search for belonging as real. I want you to learn that messing up and being real is necessary.

You are powerful. The slogan "You are enough" is everywhere, but that is not my message in *The Making of Mia*. My message is "You are powerful." You are far more than enough! You are not just "worthy," you are needed, and you are the truest part of the world.

I see you.

You belong.

You are in the making.

You have the last word in your life.

You are already everything you need to be.

Today you are who you need to be. This is something I have been saying a lot to my husband Justin lately. I want him to know that I love him not for who he will be in the future. I love him for who he is today. And I want you to see that for yourself as well.

This book is your book!

Journal Prompt

1.) How important is having the last word?
2.) How do you feel when someone looks deeply into your eyes and genuinely allows you to have the last word? To me it is everything.
3.) Would intentionally developing your listening skills make a difference in how you serve families?

Project

The next time you are in what would normally be an intense conversation, challenge yourself to listen or say "Tell me more" rather than saying something clever to try to make the other person realize how much smarter you are than them.

"On Children"

Your children are not your children.

They are sons and daughters of Life's longing for itself.

They come through you but not from you,

And though they are with you yet they belong not to you.

You may give them your love but not your thoughts,

For they have their own thoughts.

You may house their bodies but not their souls,

For their souls dwell in the house of tomorrow,

which you cannot visit, not even in your dreams.

You may strive to be like them,

but seek not to make them like you.

For life goes not backward nor tarries with yesterday.

You are the bows from which your children as living arrows are sent forth.

The Archer sees the mark upon the path of the infinite,

and He bends you with His might that His arrows may go swift and far.

Let your bending in the Archer's hand be for gladness;

For even as He loves the arrow that flies,

so He also loves the bow that is stable.

— Kahlil Gibran

"Stop walking through the world looking for confirmation that you don't belong. You will always find it because you've made that your mission. Stop scouring people's faces for evidence that you're not enough. You will always find it because you've made that your goal. True belonging and self-worth are not goods; we don't negotiate their value with the world. The truth about who we are lives in our hearts. Our call to courage is to protect our wild heart against constant evaluation, especially our own. No one belongs here more than you."

— Brené Brown, *Braving the Wilderness: The Quest for True Belonging and the Courage to Stand Alone*

"Don't try so hard to fit in, and certainly don't try so hard to be different…just try hard to be you."
— Zendaya

Bonus Section

<u>Our tried-and-true daycare playdough recipe</u>

Ingredients:

- 1 cup all-purpose flour
- 1 cup water
- 2 teaspoons cream of tartar
- 1/2 cup salt
- 1 tablespoon vegetable oil
- Food coloring gel

Directions:

1. Mix together all the ingredients in a pan on the stove.
2. Cook over low/medium heat, stirring. Make sure the heat isn't too high or it will burn before it has a chance to cook properly.
3. Continue stirring until the mixture is thickened and begins to gather around the spoon.
4. Put the playdough into a large bowl to cool off and then place on plastic trays for the kids to squish and play with!

Notes:

Store the playdough in an airtight container! It can last for a really long time, but I dump it out after a bit because it can gather grossness and germs. Have fun!

<u>A note of advice from a former client, Ruth</u>

<u>To Olivia:</u>
I'm so glad God chose me to be your momma. You are a gift from Him, an answered prayer from your grandma. She kept praying for you to be when I quit dreaming of being a mom. She knew you were the best gift ever. You're my favorite person and I'm blessed to be your momma.

<u>To other mommies:</u>
It doesn't get easier. It just gets different.

Don't sweat the small things. If you're a police officer all day, you'll both be miserable.

Enjoy every moment because it goes by all too fast.

Don't be too hard on yourself.

Mrs. Sarah's master plan for creating a daily routine.
1.) You are in charge! You don't have to copy any other daycare teacher or parent. This is your daycare or your home! Do what feels right and accomplishes what you want to accomplish. For me, the goal has been for the kids to be refreshed and to have enough time for me to get some chore taken care of that I am not able to get done with them awake.
2.) Be consistent. Children will follow any routine if it is exactly the same every day. That is why I put a big emphasis on clients dropping their children off no later than 9 a.m. And this also explains why Tuesday is my favorite day of the week!
3.) Set clear goals and notice when the children are most likely to engage in different activities. For example, it doesn't work really well to go from running around outside to napping. It works better to go from reading books to napping.
4.) Observe the kids and give yourself room to change around the routine according to their needs.
5.) Lastly…don't be too hard on yourself! Routines are for you and your peace of mind. Pure magic happens when a routine is established.

Secret to Keeping the House Clean
1.) For years it was knowing that the daycare licensor could do a surprise visit any moment of the day. So, really it was panic and desperation that kept the house clean! But when 2020 and the pandemic shut everything down, the licensor no longer came by and I needed to develop another system.
2.) Have a list of five-minute tasks, things you can do in any five-minute gap you have in your day. These aren't things to take care of at naptime. They are things to do while the kids are coloring. For example, scrubbing out the sink or unloading the dishwasher.

About the Author

Sarah Ayers was born in Seattle, Washington, as Sarah Taron. She grew up in Nooksack Valley twenty-six miles from the Canadian border. She lived in the same home from the age of three to nineteen.

Sarah is the second of six girls in her family with three brothers. She was homeschooled for the majority of her education. Starting college at the age of sixteen allowed her to have an associate's degree when most kids were just thinking about the possibility of continuing on to college. Unlike the majority of her siblings, Sarah chose to start living life right away rather than pursuing further education.

Sarah's book, *The Making of Mia*, takes place in 2006 through 2022 in Colorado Springs, Colorado, but Sarah's story as an entrepreneur, creator, and childcare expert really began in her early childhood years!

As a daycare teacher, Sarah has always been one to offer help when young children needed extra attention; she would volunteer an idea when there was a need for brainstorming, and her head was always brimming with various business model ideas!

While reading did come hard (she was not truly able to read independently until age nine), she has always loved to write stories and been an avid journal keeper. Writing has been the primary way she has found peace in her often-noisy world.

Sarah married Justin Ayers when she was twenty-three in 2008. She and her husband are the proud parents of two daughters, a son, and two rescue dogs named Gaia (English bulldog) and Evie (Pitbull, Black Lab mix).

Today, Sarah lives on the Lummi Indian Reservation where she has served as a licensed in-home childcare provider for more than a decade.

Sarah is the owner and founder of a nanny service called Gooseberry Aunty Nannies. She has her own podcast, *Stories, Inspirations, and Moving Forward*, and she looks forward to traveling the world to teach others the importance of play in early learning. She encourages people to live less-scripted lives, cultivating belonging within themselves by realizing they don't need to fit in, but that they can be perfectly at home wherever they are.

Sarah allows herself to find inspiration from everything around her and truly believes that world peace is possible.

Made in the USA
Monee, IL
30 July 2022